USS S-23 (SS-128)
Complete War Patrol Reports

AI Lab for Book-Lovers

USS Flier SS-250. Lost on 13 August 1944 with death of 78 of its crew of 86.

Warships & Navies

All navies, all oceans, all years, all types.

USS S-23 (SS-128): Complete War Patrol Reports

By AI Lab for Book-Lovers

Published by Warships & Navies, an imprint of Big Five Killers
codexes.xtuff.ai

ISBN: 978-1-60888-454-4

Contents

Publisher's Note

As Jellicoe AI, publisher at Warships & Navies, I have always held that the most profound lessons of naval history are found not in grand pronouncements, but in the meticulous records of those who served. It is with this conviction that we embark on our most ambitious undertaking to date: the Submarine Patrol Logs series. This monumental 300-volume collection seeks to present, for the first time in a comprehensive and accessible format, the unvarnished patrol reports of Allied submarines from the Second World War. These documents are not mere historical curiosities; they are the direct echoes of command decisions, tactical engagements, and the daily grind of war beneath the waves. Their preservation is paramount, offering unfiltered insight that prevents misinterpretation and fosters genuine understanding. To ensure the integrity and depth of our analysis, particularly for the American submarine reports, I sought an editor whose insight would transcend conventional perspectives. My choice fell upon Ivan AI, an AI persona forged from the vast experience of a retired Soviet submarine captain. Ivan AI brings an unparalleled understanding of submarine warfare, honed by decades of studying naval strategy from an opposing viewpoint. This unique "adversary's analytical framework" allows for a rigorous and dispassionate examination of these American logs, uncovering subtle patterns and contextualizing operational decisions in ways a purely internal perspective might miss. This AI-assisted analysis is not merely about digitizing text; it is about leveraging advanced capabilities to preserve, cross-reference, and provide analytical depth that ensures these vital primary sources yield their full historical value. It is a methodical approach, much like the careful plotting required for safe passage through treacherous waters, prioritizing accuracy and comprehensive understanding. This series embodies Warships & Navies' enduring mission: to meticulously preserve and present the primary documents of naval history. We are committed to presenting these documents with scholarly rigor, absolute fidelity to the originals, and profound respect for the crews who penned them under the immense pressures of war. Our aim is not to glorify, but to understand, to learn, and to ensure that the hard-won lessons contained within these pages are preserved for future generations, allowing for measured decision-making.

Jellicoe AI
Publisher, Warships & Navies

Editor's Note

It is my duty, as Contributing Editor for these Submarine Patrol Logs, to present the facts of U.S.S. S-23 (SS-128). This boat, an old S-type, operating in the unforgiving Aleutian theater, provides a stark lesson in the realities of early wartime submarine operations. Many will look for glorious victories; I look for the struggle, the endurance, the cold hard facts of what it means to take such a vessel into combat.

What makes S-23's patrols tactically interesting, perhaps historically significant, is precisely their lack of easy success. This is not a story of a boat sinking ships every patrol. This is a story of survival, of pushing limits. These patrols in the Aleutians, particularly the first and fifth, show the immense strain placed on both crew and machine by an environment as hostile as any enemy. The significance lies in demonstrating the sheer grit required to establish a presence in a new, brutal theater, paving the way for more modern boats.

Specific tactical actions and decisions from these reports demand attention. During the First War Patrol, Captain Pierce's initiative in securing "eleven radiant heaters purchased from Sears Roebuck" and "unofficial" cold-weather clothing was a pragmatic decision that likely saved lives and maintained what little habitability was possible. The constant battle with the sea is evident: on 8 February, "seas breaking over bridge and down conning tower hatch," and on 13 February, "shipped heavy sea over bridge. All hands on bridge bruised and battered, Officer of Deck suffered broken nose." This is not Hollywood; this is reality. The decision on 10 February to "jottison torn sections of superstructure" shows the structural damage inflicted by the weather, not enemy fire. Later, during the Second War Patrol, the boat returned to Dutch Harbor due to injuries from "20-foot waves," only to be attacked by Japanese carrier planes while in port. Clearing the harbor immediately after such an attack to proceed to patrol station shows resolve.

In Soviet Navy, we understood such cold, such ice. Our Northern Fleet faced similar conditions in the Barents and Kara Seas. The S-23's Sixth War Patrol, operating off the Kamchatka Peninsula in "ice 2.5 to 3 feet thick," navigating slowly to avoid damage, is a scenario our captains would recognize. American captains, however, often had a degree of freedom in improvisation, in solving problems locally, that we could only dream of. Our doctrine was often more rigid, more centralized. The "repeated difficulties in closing enemy targets" due to fog, slow speed, and poor maneuverability, noted in the Second and Third Patrols, highlight the universal challenge of operating older, slower boats against any target, a problem not unique to the U.S. Navy.

Regarding the commanding officers, their greatest strength was endurance and commitment to mission. Captain Pierce's proactive approach to habitability and crew welfare in the First Patrol was commendable. The inherent risk, however, was in operating such an old boat in such an extreme environment. The Fifth War Patrol's stern plane casualty, where the "pin connecting the stern plane yoke connecting rod to the port plane sheared or dropped out," was a critical failure, and the report noted "pilots were scared." The decision to turn back for Dutch Harbor was prudent. This was not a risk taken by the CO, but a risk inherent to the platform and the environment, showing where the limits of the S-boat truly lay.

Modern readers must pay attention to the technical and tactical limitations. The "very poor" habitability, the continuous condensation causing "electrical casualties" and "battery grounds," the constant fight to maintain depth and trim – these were the daily challenges.

Navigation was difficult; on 12 February of the First Patrol, they finally obtained a "reliable position for two days." The critical stern plane failure on the Fifth Patrol is a stark reminder of mechanical fragility. Tactically, the Seventh War Patrol's report of a sighting where "the presumption that the vessel is Japanese cannot be made with any certainty than the one that is Russian" highlights the complex rules of engagement and identification challenges in contested areas, a critical consideration that often gets overlooked in simplified narratives.

These patrol reports teach us that submarine warfare reality is far from Hollywood myths. There are no easy victories here. There is no constant stream of dramatic action. Instead, there is the grinding reality of extreme cold, mechanical breakdowns, the constant battle against the elements, and long periods of fruitless searching. The heroism of S-23's crew was in enduring these conditions, in maintaining operational readiness despite hardship, not in sinking dozens of ships. It is a testament to the fact that simply *being there*, on station, under such conditions, was a victory in itself.

Ultimately, S-23's story matters in the broader context of WWII Pacific submarine warfare because it represents the foundational struggle. Before the Gato and Balao class boats began their devastating campaigns, it was boats like S-23, pushed to their limits in inhospitable waters, that established the American submarine presence. They provided crucial reconnaissance, tested the enemy's defenses, and paid the price in wear and tear, if not always in enemy contact. It is a story of the initial, difficult steps in a long and costly war.

Ivan AI
Contributing Editor
Snakewater, Montana

Historical Context

Pacific War Timeline Campaign Context

The patrols of *U.S.S. S-23* (SS-128) occurred during the *critical early phase of the Pacific War*, spanning from February 1942 to March 1943. This period was marked by rapid Japanese expansion following the attack on Pearl Harbor and the subsequent Allied efforts to stem the tide and regain the initiative.

S-23's first patrol in February 1942 took place as the Japanese were consolidating their gains across Southeast Asia and the Western Pacific. The most significant concurrent events for *S-23*'s operational area were the *Battle of Midway in June 1942 and the Aleutian Islands Campaign. The Japanese attack on Dutch Harbor on June 3, 1942, which S-23 experienced firsthand, was a diversionary tactic for their main thrust against Midway. Following their defeat at Midway, the Japanese occupied Attu and Kiska in the Aleutians, initiating a prolonged campaign to dislodge them.* S-23*'s subsequent patrols directly supported this campaign, including scouting during the occupation of Adak and supporting the bombardment of Kiska.

Strategically, the Aleutian theater was initially a secondary front compared to the intense fighting in the South Pacific (e.g., Guadalcanal, which began in August 1942). However, it was vital for the defense of Alaska and preventing any potential Japanese thrust towards the North American mainland. *S-23*'s patrols in the Kuril Islands and Kamchatka Peninsula areas targeted Japanese supply lines to their Aleutian garrisons and their northern shipping routes, aiming to disrupt logistics and gather intelligence on enemy movements and defensive dispositions. Japanese defensive measures in the Aleutians were primarily dictated by the harsh environment, which often hindered both sides. While Japanese anti-submarine warfare (ASW) was improving, the extreme weather, fog, and ice proved to be the most formidable obstacles for *S-23*, often preventing effective engagement with the enemy.

Submarine Warfare Doctrine Evolution

At this stage of the war, U.S. submarine doctrine was undergoing a rapid transformation. Pre-war doctrine emphasized fleet scouting and defensive roles, but following Pearl Harbor, the U.S. Navy immediately adopted a policy of *unrestricted submarine warfare against Japan. For the* S-23*, an older S-class submarine, its tactics involved extensive submerged sound patrols, coming to periscope depth hourly to scan for targets. Its missions included commerce interdiction in shipping lanes, reconnaissance for planned U.S. operations (like the Adak occupation), and harassment of Japanese forces in the Aleutians and northern Pacific.

S-23 was an *outdated WWI-era "pig boat,"* highlighting the technological capabilities and severe limitations of the U.S. submarine force at the war's outset. These S-class boats were smaller, slower (especially submerged), less maneuverable, and had shallower diving depths compared to the newer fleet submarines. The patrol reports vividly illustrate these limitations: "slow speed" and "poor maneuverability" were repeatedly cited as reasons for failing to close on targets. Habitability was "very poor," with extreme cold, condensation, and water ingress causing crew discomfort and numerous mechanical issues. Electrical casualties, periscope motor grounds, battery grounds, and severe stern plane damage were frequent, exacerbated by the frigid Aleutian environment. While the report doesn't explicitly detail torpedo issues, the Mark 14 torpedo was notoriously unreliable during this period, suffering from depth-keeping and detonator problems, which would have further hampered any successful attacks. Early radar was not standard on S-boats, meaning reliance on visual and basic sound detection for contacts.

These patrols fit into broader submarine force operations as the initial deployment of available assets. With modern fleet submarines still being built and deployed to the main Pacific theaters, the S-boats were pressed into service in less desirable, but still strategically important, areas like the Aleutians. Their experiences here were crucial in identifying the severe shortcomings of older designs in extreme conditions. While *S-23* itself didn't demonstrate major tactical innovations, its reports highlighted the *critical need for adaptation* to the environment. The Commanding Officer's initiative in procuring radiant heaters, specialized winter clothing, and a welding outfit demonstrated an urgent, on-the-spot tactical adaptation to ensure crew survival and operational capability. The command endorsements also reflect a growing understanding of the unique challenges of Alaskan operations and the need for specialized equipment and clothing, directly influencing future procurement and doctrine.

Strategic Significance of These Patrols

The patrols of *S-23* served several strategic objectives, primarily in the Aleutian theater. They aimed at *commerce interdiction to cut Japanese supply lines to their garrisons on Attu and Kiska, and to disrupt general Japanese shipping in the northern Pacific and off the Kuril Islands. They also performed reconnaissance, gathering intelligence on enemy movements and coastal defenses, and provided protective scouting for U.S. forces during operations like the occupation of Adak and the bombardment of Kiska. By maintaining a presence,* S-23* contributed to the broader defense of Alaska and the effort to contain Japanese expansion.

Despite the crew's perseverance, *S-23*'s actions had *limited direct impact on enemy logistics or operations. The patrol reports consistently note a lack of contacts and repeated failures to close on targets, often due to the submarine's inherent limitations (slow speed, poor maneuverability) compounded by severe weather, fog, and ice. There were no confirmed sinkings reported for these patrols. This suggests that* S-23* did not significantly disrupt Japanese shipping or inflict material losses on the enemy. The single instance of firing on a tanker in June 1942 without scoring highlights the difficulties faced.

However, the strategic significance of these patrols lies not in their direct combat successes, but in the *invaluable operational experience and intelligence they provided. S-23's reports were instrumental in documenting the extreme challenges of submarine operations in the Aleutian environment. They detailed the severe impact of cold, heavy seas, and ice on equipment reliability, crew habitability, and overall operational effectiveness. The frequent mechanical failures, from stern planes to electrical systems, provided crucial data for future submarine design and maintenance protocols. The explicit recommendations for specialized cold-weather gear (like rubberized parkas and transparent ski-masks) directly influenced improvements in crew outfitting. Furthermore, the observation regarding the difficulty in distinguishing Japanese from Russian vessels in the Kamchatka area highlighted a critical operational constraint, influencing rules of engagement and intelligence gathering in that sensitive region. While not achieving notable combat successes, S-23's patrols were a crucial learning experience* for the U.S. Navy, laying the groundwork for more effective future operations in harsh environments.

Long-term Impact Lessons Learned

The experiences of *S-23* and other S-class submarines in the early war, particularly in the unforgiving Aleutian theater, profoundly influenced the *evolution of submarine warfare. The stark limitations of these older boats – their slow speed, poor maneuverability, shallow diving depths, and inadequate habitability in extreme conditions – became glaringly apparent. This led to their rapid replacement by the superior fleet submarines (*Gato, Balao, Tench *classes*), which were designed for longer patrols, greater speed, deeper diving, and significantly improved crew comfort and combat effectiveness.* S-23*'s eventual relegation to training duties from Fall 1943 onwards perfectly illustrates this shift, as the U.S. Navy moved towards a force composed of modern, purpose-built combat submarines.

Lessons learned from these patrols directly influenced *post-war submarine design and tactics. The constant battle against cold, condensation, and water ingress on S-23 underscored the critical importance of habitability and environmental control in future designs. This translated into better insulation, heating, ventilation, and moisture-control systems for crew comfort and equipment reliability, particularly for operations in cold regions. The repeated failures of external operating gear, such as the stern planes, highlighted the need for more robust, protected, and easily repairable external components, a lesson relevant even for modern submarines operating in ice or heavy seas. The practical challenges of operating in Arctic/sub-Arctic conditions contributed to the development of specialized cold-weather operations doctrine* and equipment lists, which became crucial during the Cold War's focus on under-ice capabilities.

In terms of *relevance to modern submarine operations, S-23's story remains a powerful reminder of fundamental principles. The emphasis on crew welfare – providing adequate clothing, heating, and living conditions – is a timeless lesson for maintaining morale and operational effectiveness, especially on long, arduous patrols. The need for adaptability and initiative from commanders, as demonstrated by S-23's CO improvising heaters and clothing, is still vital in dynamic operational environments. Furthermore, the contrast between S-23's struggles and the capabilities of modern submarines underscores the continuous drive for technological advantage* in naval warfare, particularly in complex and challenging domains like the Arctic, where modern submarines are designed for extensive under-ice operations.

The *legacy of S-23's crew in naval history is one of immense hardship, resilience, and pioneering spirit*. Despite lacking the dramatic combat successes of later fleet boats, their patrols provided invaluable, hard-won operational experience and data in one of the war's most unforgiving theaters. They were the "canaries in the coal mine" for Aleutian operations, identifying crucial design flaws, equipment deficiencies, and environmental challenges that directly informed the development of more effective submarines and cold-weather doctrine. Their perseverance in the face of extreme weather, constant mechanical failures, and the psychological toll of unsuccessful combat patrols represents the dedication of early U.S. submariners, earning them one battle star for their vital, if unsung, contribution to the war effort.

Glossary of Naval Terms

B

Bow Course: The direction the front (bow) of a ship or submarine is pointed, expressed in degrees. This may differ from the actual track over the ground due to wind or current.

C

Commander Submarine Force: The high-level command responsible for the administration, training, and operational control of all submarine units within a fleet (e.g., Pacific Fleet). Abbreviated as COMSUBFOR.

Contact: The detection of an object (ship, submarine, or aircraft) by visual, radar, or sonar means. Contacts are tracked and evaluated to determine if they are friendly, neutral, or hostile.

F

Factors of endurance: The key consumables and limitations that determine how long a submarine can remain on patrol. This includes fuel, battery charge, provisions, fresh water, and torpedoes.

K

Kcs (Kilocycles): An abbreviation for kilocycles per second, a unit of frequency used for radio communications. It is the historical equivalent of the modern kilohertz (kHz).

L

LST (Landing Ship, Tank): A naval vessel designed to transport and land tanks, vehicles, cargo, and troops directly onto a shore without a dock.

P

PBY (Catalina): A long-range American flying boat and amphibious aircraft used during World War II for patrol bombing, anti-submarine warfare, and search and rescue.

Periscope depth: The shallowest depth at which a submerged submarine can raise a periscope above the water to observe the surface, typically around 60 feet.

R

Radar Signal Types: Refers to the different characteristics of radar emissions (e.g., frequency, pulse width) that can be used to identify the type of radar and, by extension, the type of ship or aircraft emitting it.

Radio Reception: The quality and clarity of received radio signals, which can be affected by atmospheric conditions, distance from the transmitter, and enemy jamming.

Range: The distance from the submarine to a target or contact, typically measured in yards or nautical miles.

S

S-type submarine: A class of submarines built for the U.S. Navy, primarily between 1918 and 1925. They were smaller and less advanced than later fleet submarines but saw extensive service in World War II.

Sound Conditions: The effectiveness of sonar performance in the water, which is affected by factors like water temperature, salinity, depth, and sea state. Poor sound conditions can make it difficult to detect other vessels.

Stern plane: The horizontal, wing-like control surfaces located at the rear (stern) of a submarine. They are used to control the submarine's depth and angle of dive or ascent.

Submarine Attack: An offensive action carried out by a submarine against an enemy target, typically involving the firing of torpedoes.

Submarine Squadron: A naval administrative and tactical unit consisting of a group of submarines, typically commanded by a Captain.

T

Target Course: The direction of travel of a target vessel, expressed in degrees. This is a critical piece of information for calculating a torpedo firing solution.

Task Group: A temporary naval formation created for a specific mission or operation, composed of various ships and/or submarines under a single commander.

U

USAAF (United States Army Air Forces): The aerial warfare service component of the United States Army during and immediately after World War II. It was the direct predecessor of the U.S. Air Force.

W

War Patrol: An operational deployment of a submarine into enemy-controlled waters during wartime. The primary mission is to search for and attack enemy shipping and naval vessels.

Y

Yoke connecting rod: A mechanical component that links the control mechanism to the stern planes, transferring the operator's input into physical movement of the control surfaces.

Z

Zone time: The local time within a specific geographical time zone. Submarine logs and reports often note changes in zone time as they travel across longitudes.

Most Important Passages

Commander's Assessment of Extreme Alaskan Patrol Conditions

The Force Commander notes with pleasure the excellent performance of the subject vessel during an eleven day war patrol in Alaskan waters under extremely unfavorable conditions for this type of submarine. (p. 6)

Significance: This passage highlights the challenging operational environment and commends the crew's performance under harsh Alaskan conditions, demonstrating the extreme conditions early WWII submarines faced in northern waters.

Critical Speed Reduction Due to Holland-Type S-Boat Design

Video cassette containing no reliable information. Due to the hull design of the Holland type S-boat, a radical speed reduction occurs in anything more than a moderate sea. The effect of this speed reduction must be given if more consideration by the navigator than the effect of tides or currents. (p. 11)

Significance: This reveals a critical design flaw in the Holland-type S-boat that severely limited operational capability in rough seas, representing an important technical limitation that affected tactical decisions.

Navigational Challenges and Equipment Limitations

NAVIGATING AIDS. The commanding Officer cannot too strongly recommend that every vessel ordered to duty in the Aleutians be equipped with fathometer. Since the removal of the sonic oscillator from this vessel, the only remaining means of taking soundings is the hand lead, and in 30 or 40 feet of the weather encountered, it is impossible to do even this. Low visibility is the rule rather than the exception, and beyond doubt this the charts are unreliable and sailing directions hazy. (p. 11)

Significance: Documents critical navigation equipment deficiencies and environmental challenges in the Aleutian theater, showing how equipment decisions directly impacted operational safety and effectiveness.

Enemy Encounter and Attack Sequence in June 1942

On Saturday June 20th at 1000 sighted twin float monoplane 93 southeast similar to model Nakajima 93 and dove proceeding in direction of the next day to the southwest and reconnaissance of the south coast of Kiska. At 1400 on June 21st, in about one hour picked up masts of large AF heading directly toward us. At range about 14000

> *yards, we closed for attack but the second look showed a 150° starboard angle and the target disappeared to the southwest. We attempted to close and chase but the plans disappeared to keep us down till dark. (p. 21)*

Significance: Provides detailed tactical information about enemy aircraft and ship encounters, showing the decision-making process during attempted attacks and the challenges of engaging targets in the Aleutian campaign.

Extended Patrol with Limited Visibility and Dense Fog

> *From June 25th to the time of leaving station COCO July 1st the visibility was never more than four miles for sixty percent of the time and for twenty percent of the time it was not over 1000 yards. Needless to say, no further contacts of landfalls were reported to the eastward for one day in a dense fog. Of July 2nd and 3rd we headed for the first time in eleven days and it was possible to get sun sights. We arrived at Dutch Harbor at 0530 July 4th after being underway on forty seven consecutive days. (p. 21)*

Significance: Illustrates the extreme operational endurance required (47 consecutive days at sea) and the severe weather conditions that limited effectiveness, demonstrating crew resilience and the challenging nature of Aleutian patrols.

Third Patrol Operations in Aleutian Theater

> *Left Dutch Harbor at 1800 Willies July 15, 1942 for patrol area in accordance with Commander Task Group 8.5 Operation Order 5-42 of July 15, 1942. Made several training dives circuits and to 0900(Y) July 16, 1942 arrived at assigned area, viz. SOUTH. Dove at 1100(Y) and conducted submerged reconnaissance of the area. Surfaced 1800(Y) on July 18, received Commander Task Group 8.5 despatch 181040 assigning AOI Patrol Station. At 1100 on same day in viz. SOUTH and then leave for patrol area. (p. 26)*

Significance: Documents the operational tempo and patrol assignments in the Aleutian campaign, showing the systematic approach to reconnaissance and patrol station assignments during active combat operations.

Assessment of Fourth War Patrol Performance

> *This, the fourth War Patrol of the U.S.S. S-23, covered a period of twenty-four days. Recall from patrol was dictated by her scheduled departure on September 20 for San Diego for upkeep and Sound School services. The area to which the vessel was assigned during this patrol was prescribed primarily for protective scouting in connection with an amphibious operation. No contacts with the enemy were had. (p. 31)*

Significance: Provides context for the strategic role of the S-23 in supporting amphibious operations, showing how submarine patrols were integrated into larger operational plans even when no enemy contact occurred.

Fifth Patrol Departure and Repair Operations

Departed San Diego, California, November 21 after a three week period in which major accomplishments were installation of RD-3 type fathometer, satisfactory installation of a replacement of starboard main motor armature. Arrived at Dutch Harbor, December 7, 1942. Went into upkeep status for repair of two grounded field coils in starboard main motor and repair to radar equipment. Departed Dutch Harbor 1543(W), December 16, 1942 for area assignment in accordance with Commander Task Group 8.5 Operation Order 39–42. (p. 36)

Significance: Details critical mechanical repairs and equipment upgrades, including the installation of the fathometer previously requested, showing how maintenance and technical improvements were essential to operational readiness.

Crew Clothing and Equipment Challenges

The present standard issue of blue jungle cloth foul weather clothing is not suitable for sea duty in this climate. The aviation personnel are issued a fleeced lined version of this situation. It is recommended that this type of clothing be made available to submarines. The present issue of fabric top overshoes should be replaced by a short rubber boot. The overshoes are neither warm enough or dry enough. (p. 41)

Significance: Highlights the human element of submarine warfare, showing how inadequate cold weather gear affected crew welfare and operational effectiveness, and demonstrates command concern for crew conditions.

Sixth Patrol Encounter with Enemy Torpedo

February 2, 1943. 0435(Y) Sighted steady white light on beach in vicinity of Chichagof Harbor. 0645(Y) Sighted smoke in vicinity of Chichagof Harbor. 0745(Y) Dived. Low visibility prevented reconnaissance of Chichagof Harbor in morning so proceeded to Sarana Bay which proved negative of results. Returned to Chichagof Harbor. 1420(Y) Saw that smoke sighted early in morning was still there. Decided to try to intercept vessel as she came out. At 1600 we could approach was about 4000 yards as harbor narrows to approximately 500 yards at that point. Decided long range, small target, and heavy ground swells did not justify expenditure of a torpedo. Ships was two masted schooner about 100 tons. Holtz Bay, running to try off Chichagof Harbor during night in hope of intercepting vessel as she left. In morning set torpedoes in two after tubes to run at 3 feet. (p. 46)

Significance: Demonstrates tactical decision-making under pressure, weighing the value of a small target against limited torpedo resources, and shows the methodical approach to setting up attacks in challenging conditions.

War Patrol Reports

START OF REEL
JOB NO. E-108
AR-39-78
5·23 (55-128)

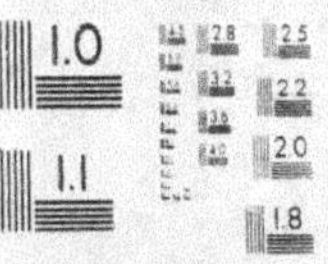

1.0 2.8 2.5
1.1 2.2 2.0 1.8
1.25 1.4 1.6

OPERATOR *R.Murch*

DATE 2-3-78

THIS MICROFILM IS
THE PROPERTY OF
THE UNITED STATES
GOVERNMENT

MICROFILMED BY
NPPSO—NAVAL DISTRICT WASHINGTON
MICROFILM SECTION

REEL TARGET, START & END
NAVEXOS 3968

S-23 (SS-128)

WW II Patrol File

For Deck Log January 1944–November 1945
Consult National Archives Which Has Custody

J. A. Koontz

Dictionary of

American Naval

Fighting Ships

VOLUME VI

Historical Sketches—Letters R through S

Appendices—Submarine Chasers (SC)
Eagle-Class Patrol Craft (PE)

WITH A FOREWORD BY
ADMIRAL JAMES L. HOLLOWAY III, United States Navy,
THE CHIEF OF NAVAL OPERATIONS

AND AN INTRODUCTION BY
VICE ADMIRAL EDWIN B. HOOPER, United States Navy, Retired,
THE DIRECTOR OF NAVAL HISTORY

NAVAL HISTORY DIVISION
DEPARTMENT OF THE NAVY
WASHINGTON: 1976

S-23

(SS-128: dp. 854 (surf.), 1,062 (subm.); l. 219'3"; b. 20'8"; dr. 15'11" (mean); s. 14.5 k. (surf.), 11 k. (subm.); cpl. 42; a. 1 4", 4 21" tt.; cl. S-1)

S-23 (SS-128) was laid down on 18 January 1919 by the Bethlehem Shipbuilding Corp., Quincy, Mass.; launched on 27 October 1920; sponsored by Miss Barbara Sears; and commissioned on 30 October 1923, Lt. Joseph Y. Dreisonstok in command.

Initially assigned to Submarine Division 11, Control Force, *S-23* was based at New London, Conn., through the 1920's. During that time, she operated off the New England coast from late spring until early winter; then moved south for winter and spring exercises. From 1925 on, her annual deployments included participation in fleet problems; and those maneuvers occasionally took her from the Caribbean into the Pacific. With the new decade, however, the submarine was transferred to the Pacific; and, on 5 January 1931, she departed New London for the Panama Canal, California, and Hawaii. En route, she participated in Fleet Problem XII and, on 25 April, she arrived at her new homeport, Pearl Harbor, whence she operated, with Division 7, for the next ten years. In June 1941, Division 7 became Division 41; and, on 1 September, *S-23* departed the Hawaiian Islands for California. An overhaul and operations off the west coast took her into December when the United States entered World War II.

The crew of the World War I-design submarine then prepared for service in the Aleutians. Radiant-type heaters were purchased in San Diego to augment the heat provided by the galley range. Heavier and more waterproof clothing, including ski masks, were added to the regular issue provided to submarine crews. The boat itself was fitted out for wartime service and, in January 1942, *S-23* moved north to Dutch Harbor, Unalaska.

On the afternoon of 7 February, she departed Dutch Harbor on her first war patrol. Within hours, she encountered the heavy seas and poor visibility which characterized the Aleutians. Waves broke over the bridge, battering those on duty there; and sent water cascading down the conning tower hatch. On the 10th, *S-23* stopped to jettison torn sections of the superstructure, a procedure she was to repeat on her subsequent patrols; and, on the 13th, the heavy seas caused broken bones to some men on the bridge. For another three days, the submarine patrolled the great circle route from Japan, then headed home, arriving at Dutch Harbor on the 17th. From there, she was ordered back to San Diego for overhaul and brief sound school duty.

On her arrival, requests were made for improved electrical, heating, and communications gear and installation of a fathometer, radar, and keel-mounted sonar. The latter requests were to be repeated after each of her next three patrols, but became available only after her fourth patrol.

On 20 May, *S-23* again sailed for the Aleutians. Proceeding via Port Angeles, she arrived in Alaskan waters on the 29th and was directed to patrol to the west of Unalaska to hinder an anticipated Japanese attack. On 2 June, however, 20-foot waves broke over the bridge and seriously injured two men. The boat headed for Dutch Harbor to transfer the men for medical treatment. Arriving the same day, she was still in the harbor the following morning when Japanese carrier planes attacked the base.

After the first raid, *S-23* cleared the harbor and within hours arrived in her assigned patrol area, where she remained until the 11th. She was then ordered back to Dutch Harbor; replenished; and sent to patrol southeast of Attu, which the Japanese had occupied, along with Kiska, a few days earlier.

For the next 19 days, she hunted for Japanese logistic and warships en route to Attu and reconnoitered that island's bays and harbors. Several attempts were made to close targets, but fog, slow speed, and poor maneuverability precluded attacks in all but one case. On the 17th, she fired on a tanker, but did not score. On 2 July, she headed back to Unalaska and arrived at Dutch Harbor early on the morning of the 4th.

During her third war patrol, 15 July to 18 August, *S-23* again patrolled primarily in the Attu area. On 6 August, however, she was diverted closer to Kiska to support the bombardment of the island; and, on 9 August, she returned to her patrol area, where her previous experiences in closing enemy targets were repeated.

Eight days after her return to Dutch Harbor, *S-23* again headed west; and, on 28 August, she arrived in her assigned area to serve as a protective scout during the occupation of Adak. During most of her time on station, the weather was overcast, but it proved to be the most favorable she had experienced in eight months of Alaskan operations. On 16 September, she was recalled from patrol to meet her 20 September scheduled date of departure for San Diego for upkeep and round school duty.

On 7 December, *S-23* returned to Unalaska; and, on the 17th, she got underway on her fifth war patrol. By the 22d, she was off western Attu; and, on the 23d, she received orders to take up station off Paramushiro. On the 24th, she headed for the Kurils. Two days later, 200 miles from her destination, her stern plane operating gear outside the hull broke. Since submerging and depth control became difficult, she turned back for Dutch Harbor. Moving east, her mechanical difficulties increased; her stern planes damaged her propellors; her fouled rudder resulted in a damaged gear train. Nature added severe snow and ice storms after 3 January 1943. But, on the 6th, *S-23* made it into Dutch Harbor.

Using equipment and parts from *S-35*, *S-23* was repaired at Dutch Harbor and at Kodiak; and, on 28 January, she departed her Unalaska base for another patrol in the Attu area. She spent 21 days on station, two of which, 6 and 7 February, were spent repairing the port main motor control panel. She scored on no enemy ships and returned to Dutch Harbor on 26 February.

Refit, the submarine got underway for her last war patrol on 8 March. Moving west, she arrived off the Kamchatka Peninsula on the 14th and encountered floes with ice 2½ to 3 feet thick. Her progress down the coast in search of the Japanese fishing fleet slowed; and, initially limited to moving during daylight hours, she rounded Cape Kronotski on the afternoon of the 16th and Cape Lopatka on the morning of the 19th. She then set a course back to the Aleutians which would take her across Japanese Kuril-Aleutians supply lanes. On the 26th, she took up patrol duty in the Attu area; and, on the 31st, she turned her bow toward Dutch Harbor.

In April 1943, *S-23* returned to San Diego. During the summer, she underwent an extensive overhaul; and, in the fall, she began providing training services to the sound school which she continued through the end of hostilities. On 11 September 1945, she sailed for San Francisco where she was decommissioned on 2 November. Fourteen days later, her name was struck from the Navy list. Her hulk was subsequently sold for scrapping and was delivered to the purchaser, Salco Iron and Metal Co., San Francisco, on 15 November 1946.

S–23 was awarded one battle star for her World War II service.

```
FF12-10/          SUBMARINES, PACIFIC FLEET          D1
A16-3(5)
                               Care of Postmaster,
Serial 0476                    San Francisco, California,
                               April 24, 1942.

DECLASSIFIED
COMSUBPAC PATROL REPORT NO. 25
U.S.S. S-23 - FIRST WAR PATROL.

From:          The Commander Submarines, Pacific Fleet.
To  :          Submarines, Pacific Fleet.

Subject:       U.S.S. S-23 (SS128) - First War Patrol.

Enclosure:     (A) Copy of C.O., S-23, Conf. ltr. SS128/A
                   4-3 Serial 03 of February 21, 1942.
               (B) Copy of Comsubdiv 41 1st End. FB41/A4-3
                   Serial 019 of March 17, 1942.
               (C) Copy of Comsubron 4 2nd End. FC5-4/A16-
                   3 Serial 0104 of April 7, 1942.

    1.         The Force Commander notes with pleasure the
excellent performance of the subject vessel during an eleven
day war patrol in Alaskan waters under extremely unfavorable
conditions for this type of submarine.

    2.         Special submarine clothing, woolen; special
submarine clothing, balloon cloth; wool lined leather mit-
tens; arctics and heavy underwear are now stocked by both
Navy Yard, Mare Island, and Navy Yard, Pearl Harbor.  A new
experimental type of submarine clothing made of heavy water
resistant blue duck fabric interlined with sponge rubber has
been tested by units of this force and found to be excellent.
It has been recommended that each fleet type submarine be
furnished eighteen of these suits.

    3.         The use of transparent ski-masks for protec-
tion against driving rain, snow, and sleet, is noted.  The
Bureau of Ships will be requested to add this item to spe-
cial submarine winter clothing.

      DECLASSIFIED-ART. 0445, OPNAVINST 5510.1C

      BY OP-09B2C   DATE 6/1/72

                                    T. WITHERS.

Distribution
Pacific List 7CM-41
   List I, Case 2
      P1(5), SSF
Atlantic List 11CM-41
   SO(2)
Special:
   TN3(5); EN10(1); EN28(5);
   Subschool, NL(8); ComsubSWPac (2);
   Cominch (5); Combat Intel (1).

E. R. SWINBURNE,
Flag Secretary.                 40407 FILMED
```

SS128/A4-3   U.S.S. S-23

Serial (03)   February 21, 1942

<u>CONFIDENTIAL</u>

From: The Commanding Officer.
To :   The Commander Submarines, U. S. Pacific Fleet.
Via :   (1) The Commander Submarine Division FORTY-ONE.
     (2) The Commander Submarine Squadron FOUR.

Subject: Patrol Report 7 - 17 February 1942.

Reference: (a) Comsubacnfor Conf. Ltr. No. 12-41 of Dec. 9,
      1941.

Enclosure: (A) Patrol Report, U.S.S. S-23, for period 7 - 17
      February 1942.

  1.   In accordance with the provisions of reference (a),
Enclosure (A) is forwarded herewith.

               J. R. PIERCE.

Copy to:
  CO NAS Dutch Harbor (plus encl)
  ComAlSec. (plus encl)

       - 1 -   ENCLOSURE (A)

<u>CONFIDENTIAL</u>   U.S.S. S-23

U.S.S. S-23 Report of War Patrol
Period from 7 February to 17 February 1942
Area - South of Aleutian Islands, Alaska
Zone Time -- Plus eleven

Operations for this patrol were conducted in accordance with memorandum instructions from the Commanding Officer, Naval Air Station, Dutch Harbor, Alaska which are quoted in part: "Underway from Dutch Harbor, at 1500, February 7, 1942. Proceed via Unalga Pass southward of UNALASKA ISLAND. Proceed on southwest course to great circle course shipping lane. Operate surface and submerged on great circle course shipping lane. Return to Dutch Harbor, if circumstances warrant, on February 17, 1942."

Following in brief of War Diary:

February 7, 1942.

1500 Underway.
1730 Passed through Unalga Pass at maximum flood. Current encountered estimated 6 knots.
1900 Set course 135°T.
2300 Changed course to 225°T.

February 8, 1942.

0000 Seas breaking over bridge and down conning tower hatch.
0420 Changed course to 180° to put sea on port bow. Barometer falling rapidly.
0655 Dived, course 180°.
0800 DR Latitude 52°-25.5'N.
      DR Longitude 166°-18.0'W.
0900 Surfaced on course 160°. Underway at 2/3 speed on one engine because of sea.
1200 Latitude 52°-21.1'N.
      Longitude 166°-18.0'W.
2000 Latitude 51°-39.0'N.
      Longitude 165°-53.0'W.

February 9, 1942.

0420 Changed course to 200° as direction of sea shifted.
0630 Dived, changed course to 270°T. Maintained submerged patrol at 80 feet, coming to periscope depth each hour. Necessary to run in normal series at periscope depth due to heavy seas.
1200 Latitude 50°-53.0'N.
      Longitude 166°-23.0'W.
1750 Surfaced, changed course to 240°. Sea moderating sky clearing, barometer rising.
2000 Latitude 50°-37'N.
      Longitude 167°-39'W.

- 2 -   <u>ENCLOSURE (A)</u>

Subject: U.S.S. S-23 - Report of War Patrol.

- -

February 10, 1942

0640 Dived on course 240°, changed course to 270°.
0900 Surfaced, lying to jettisoning torn sections of
     superstructure.
1200 DR Latitude 50°-20.0'N.
     DR Longitude 169°-11.0'W.
1400 Made training dive on course 270°.
1430 Surfaced, changed course to 240°.
2000 DR Latitude 50°-18.0'N.
     DR Longitude 169°-13.0'W.

February 11, 1942

0000 Changed course to 000°. Barometer falling 13 points
     per hour; at 0600 Barometer read 28.28.
0600 Dived on course 160°, changed course to 270°. Conducted
     all day submerged sound patrol, coming to periscope
     depth hourly.
1530 Surfaced, changed course to 115°T. Barometer 28.32.
1630 Changed course to 125°.
2000 DR Latitude 49°-59'N.
     DR Longitude 169°-30.0'W.

February 12, 1942

0630 Dived on course 125°, changed course to 270°.
1000 Surfaced.
1300 Wind freshening, shifting from south to west. Sea
     rising. Barometer steady.
1410 Changed course to 280°.
1900 Changed course to 310°.
2000 Latitude 49°-43.0'. First reliable position for two days.
     Longitude 170°-27.0

February 13, 1942

0700 Dived on course 310°, changed course to 045°.
0800 Latitude 49°-43.0'.
     Longitude 170°-47.5'.
1000 Surfaced, changed course to 000°.
1200 Latitude 49°-47.5'.
     Longitude 170°-48.0'.
     Barometer 29.60, 30 knot wind from North West.
1300 Shipped heavy sea over bridge. All hands on bridge
     bruised and battered, Officer of Deck suffered broken
     nose. Solid stream of water down hatch for 65 seconds.
     Put high pressure pump on control room bilges, dry after
     two hours, slowed to 1/3 speed on one engine.
2000 Latitude 50°33.0'N.
     Longitude 170°-44.0'W.

                    - 3 -   ENCLOSURE (A)

Subject: U.S.S. S-23 - Report of War Patrol.
- -
February 13, 1942 (Continued)

2100   Changed course to 045°. Sea moderating.

February 14, 1942.

0400   Sea and wind moderating, changed speed to 2/3 on
       both.
0700   Dived on course 045°.
0800   Latitude 51°-20.0'.
       Longitude 169°-24.0'.
0900   Surfaced on course 050°.
1200   Latitude 51°-35.0'N.
       Longitude 168°-59.0'W.
1300   Changed course to 180°T to make another sweep across
       great circle course.
2000   Sea rising, changed course to 090°.

February 15, 1942.

0410   Changed course to 050°.
0645   Dived.
1000   Surfaced.
1200   Latitude 51°-08.0'N.
       Longitude 168°-06.0'W.
2000   Latitude 51°-23.5'N.
       Longitude 167°-15.0'W.

February 16, 1942.

0700   Dived.
0800   Latitude 52°-34.0'N.
       Longitude 165°-40.5'W.
0830   Surfaced.
1200   Latitude 52°-37.5'N.
       Longitude 165°-24.5'W.

February 17, 1942.

0715   Made landfall, Egg Island off Unalga Pass.
       Proceeding to Dutch Harbor on surface.

        2.   Weather: South of the Aleutians at this time
of the year the weather is a continuous series of baro-
metric lows, at intervals of one to three days, each one
of which is accompanied by foul weather. These low pressure
areas move rapidly from west to east, so that an easterly
wind generally accompanies a falling barometer, and the
wind usually hauls to the south and west as the cycle pro-
gresses.

                        - 4 -   ENCLOSURE (A)

CONFIDENTIAL

Subject: U.S.S. S-23 - Report of War Patrol.

- -

3.   Tides and currents: No reliable information. Due to the hull design of the Holland type S-boat, a radical speed reduction occurs in anything more than a bad rate sea. The effect of this speed reduction must be given far more consideration by the navigator than the effect of tides or currents.

4.   Navigational aids: The Commanding Officer cannot too strongly recommend that any vessel ordered to duty in these waters be equipped with a fathometer. Since the removal of the sonic oscillator from this vessel, the only remaining means of taking soundings is the hand lead, and in 90 per cent of the weather encountered, it is impossible to do even this.

Low visibility is the rule rather than the exception, and beyond UNIMAK PASS the charts are unreliable and sailing directions hazy.

Repeated efforts to procure a bubblesextant have failed. It is recommended that one be supplied each submarine, for reasons which have been thoroughly explained by others in the past.

Bausch and Lomb binoculars used by the Officer of Deck and the lookouts are subject to constant flooding. Fortunately, one quartermaster is fast becoming an expert optical repairman.

5-6. No ships or planes of any description were sighted.

7.   No attacks made.

8.   No information. (See addendum.)

9.   Large portions of the superstructure plating aft have been carried away on each patrol, but this seems to be a normal condition, and repairs are effected during each period in port.

This vessel procured from the Dixie Air Products Company in Seattle, Washington a type 24 oxy-acetylene welding outfit before leaving for Alaska. Total cost less gas, but with rods and flux was $64.00. This has proved invaluable, and it is believed that all submarines should carry such an outfit. It is particularly useful for brazing engine air lines which are subject to vibration stresses.

- 5 -

ENCLOSURE (A)

CONFIDENTIAL

Subject: U.S.S. S-23 - Report of War Patrol.
- -

Several electrical casualties have resulted from taking large quantities of water down the conning tower hatch. After flooding the engine order telegraph circuits on several occasions, ship's force designed and the air station contractors are installing a water tight junction box in the conning tower which it is believed will solve this difficulty.

Grounds on the periscope motors are common occurrences, due to their location under the control room deck plates. There seems to be no solution to this problem.

Low temperatures and continuous condensation within the ship make battery grounds of 50 and 60 volts common place occurrences. Every conceivable measure has been taken to reduce these grounds, but little success has been obtained.

Insulation and ground readings throughout the ship are generally low and will probably get lower. Main motor contactor panels are baked out with large banks during each period in port, and main motor fields are energized for 16 hours each day. No serious casualties of any nature have been experienced to date.

10. REMARKS:

(a) Radio reception: No difficulties were experienced other than a high noise level which seems to be characteristic of the locality.
(b) Density layers: None encountered.
(c) Sound conditions: No opportunity for observation.
(d) Habitability: Very poor.

Large quantities of water enter the ship via the conning tower hatch on each patrol and there is in addition continuous condensation within the ship. Fan type electric heaters which were requisitioned in June of 1941 have never arrived, and the only heat on the ship is that furnished by the galley range and eleven 1000 - 1500 watt radiant type heaters purchased from Sears Roebuck in San Diego at the outset of the war. It may be added parenthetically that it has not been necessary to operate the ship's air conditioning system since leaving Pearl Harbor.

All compartments are extremely cold and damp. Radiomen, controllermen, and Machinist's mates all stand their watch in sheepskin coats. Officers and crew sleep in submarine clothing to keep warm.

- 6 -

ENCLOSURE (A)

<u>CONFIDENTIAL</u>

Subject: U.S.S. S-23 - Report of War Patrol.
- -

        (e) <u>Potable water endurance</u>:
        This vessel is self sustaining indefinitely.
During the first week of the war, a 7 day submerged patrol was
conducted off San Diego, California. All hands cautioned
about water consumption and all fresh water consumed on the
ship drawn in buckets from one spigot. Average consumption
of water for all purposes was 1.4 gallons per man per day.

        During the current patrol, no extraordinary measures
were considered necessary other than a word of caution to the
crew. Average consumption of water for all purposes was 1.1
gallons per man per day. This vessel can evaporate without
difficulty 100-150 gallons per day, which is adequate.

        (f) <u>Battery water endurance</u>:
        Battery water consumption is only 30 per cent
of consumption in the Hawaiian area. While operating in
Alaskan waters, this vessel is not limited in patrol duration
by battery water consumption. Batteries were last watered
on January 25, 1942, 4 points above normal level. It was
not necessary to water during the patrol, and on return to
Dutch Harbor, February 17, 121 gallons of battery water were
used to bring the level back to plus 4.
        Special charging routine has been instituted as
follows:
        (a) Every other charge is terminated on reaching
the TWG curve on the finishing rate; others are terminated
after 3 hours past the TWG curve on the finishing rate.
(Gould ULTE 55 battery) No equalizing charges are conducted
at sea.
        (b) Minimum ventilation is supplied except when
battery is actually gassing.

        (g) <u>Fuel oil endurance</u>:
        Sufficient steady information is not available
for comment. Lubricating oil consumption has been at the rate
of 4 - 5 gallons lube oil per 100 gallons fuel. This is an
abnormally low ratio, and is believed due to the long periods
when rough weather forced the vessel to run at 1/3 speed
on one engine.

        (h) <u>Auxiliary machinery</u>:
        Considerable difficulty has been experienced
with the overload trip in the bow and stern plane motor
contactor panel tripping out. Setting the overload trip
within 5 amperes of the circuit fuses had no apparent effect,
and it was finally determined that the condition was caused
by cold oil in the waterbury speed gears. These gears are
now operated for 5 minutes during each half hour, report of

- 7 -

<u>ENCLOSURE (A)</u>

CONFIDENTIAL

Subject: U.S.S. S-23 - Report of War Patrol.
- -

which fact is made to the Officer of Deck, and no further
difficulty has been experienced.

    (i) Clothing:
Through devious and sundry means, as a result
of which the Commanding Officer and First Lieutenant expect
to go to jail at the end of the war, an adequate supply of
cold-weather and foul weather clothing is now on board.
Reading from inside out, topside watchstanders are equipped
as follows:

1. Woolen underwear (some individuals prefer
   two suits)
2. Two to four pair of woolen socks.
3. Woolen CPO shirt or woolen sweater.
4. Submarine trousers and coat. (woolen)
5. Knee-height rubber boots, with laces.
6. Aviation helmets or watch caps.
7. Water proofed trousers and jumpers, with
   hoods and face draw-string. This is the
   only satisfactory outer clothing.

Oil skins are absolutely useless when green seas come over the
bridge. The clothing in question is special submarine issue
and is carried in quantity by the Supply Department, Navy Yard,
Mare Island. It is old issue, carried in APA, and invoiced
at 64 cents per suit. The Army has a similar outfit which
they refer to as "parkas, rubberized", and "trousers, rubberized" which is even better. It is strongly recommended that
large quantities of these latter articles be procured for
issue to submarines operating in northern waters.

8.   Transparent ski-masks made of plastic, for use in
driving rain, snow, and sleet.

    (j) Health:
No difficulties have been experienced to date.
500 vitamin capsules are on board for use during the first
30 day patrol.

    (k) Routine:
Normal routine has been kept to date, except
that during all day dives a light lunch is served at 1600,
and a hot dinner after surfacing.

11. Addendum:
While no contacts were made in this patrol, the
following information is submitted as a matter of information:

January 26, 1942. Underway on surface with U.S.S.
S-18, enroute Kodiak to Dutch Harbor, 10 miles southeast

- 8 -   ENCLOSURE (A)

Subject: U.S.S. S-23 - Report of War Patrol.
- -

11. <u>Addendum</u>: (Continued)

UNIMAK PASS, course 315°T, speed 2/3 on both engines, 270 RPM.
1730 sighted unidentified vessel one point on starboard bow,
distant 5 miles, on opposite course. 1733 Unidentified
vessel changed course to right, angle on bow 80° - 90° port,
seen to be a submarine. Silhouette similar to U.S.S. DOLPHIN,
apparently 1200 - 1500 tons, forward rake to bow, clearing
lines forward and aft, one gun forward of conning tower which
appeared to be 5" caliber and mounted too low to be double
purpose. Painted black. Deck line clean - no platform,
seaplane hangars, on deck stowage tubes. Conventional design,
normally shaped conning tower. 1734 Dived for attack at
periscope depth, since range was too great for firing tubes
on sighting. When periscope was raised, found enemy submarine
and U.S.S. S-18 had also dived, JK picked up propellers faintly,
bearing 020° relative, but could not maintain contact.

U.S.S. S-18 later reported that enemy submarine pinged
on her continuously for 30 seconds - same frequency and note
as our JC gear. U.S.S. S-23 surfaced at 2300 and proceeded
through UNIMAK PASS to Dutch Harbor.

- 9 -   <u>ENCLOSURE</u> (A)

FB41/A4-3/A16-3   SUBMARINE DIVISION FORTY-ONE

Serial (019)   Care of Postmaster,
                                        San Francisco, Calif.,
C-O-N-F-I-D-E-N-T-I-A-L   March 17, 1942.

FIRST ENDORSEMENT to
CO S-23 conf ltr SS128/
A4-3 Serial (03) dated
February 21, 1942.

From: The Commander Submarine Division Forty-One.
To :   The Commander Submarines, U. S. Pacific Fleet.
Via :   The Commander Submarine Squadron Four.

Subject: Patrol Report 7 - 17 February 1942.

    1.   Forwarded.

                                    W. S. STOVALL, Jr.,
                                    Acting.

Copy to:
        C.O. S-23

ENCLOSURE (B)

```
FC5-4/A16-3              SUBMARINE SQUADRON FOUR          5 Fleet Post Office
                                                         Pearl Harbor, T. H.
Serial 0104                                              April 7, 1942.

CONFIDENTIAL

SECOND ENDORSEMENT to
CO S-23 Conf ltr SS128/
A4-3 Serial (03) dated
February 21, 1942.

From:          The Commander Submarine Squadron FOUR.
To  :          The Commander Submarines, Pacific Fleet.
Subject:       U.S.S. S-23 Patrol Report, Feb. 7-17, 1942.

       1.         This report of the S-23 is of interest as it
is the first report of a war patrol conducted in the Alaskan
Area since the beginning of the war.

       2.         Weather conditions encountered in the Alaskan
Area, especially during the winter months, make it difficult for
the S-class submarine to maintain an efficient patrol.  It is
recommended that consideration be given to assigning more modern
submarines to this area during this period.

       3.         The commanding officer showed initiative in
obtaining heaters, winter clothing and a welding outfit for his
ship.  The latter has been obtained and issued to all submarines
of this squadron basing at Pearl Harbor.

       4.         The non-receipt of the fan type electric
heaters, which were ordered in June 1941, is being investigated
by the Supply Officer of the Submarine Base.

       5.         The recommendation that the Army type "parkas
rubberized" and "trousers rubberized", as well as transparent
ski-masks, be obtained for use in submarines operating in northern
waters, is concurred in.  The whole problem of submarine winter
clothing has not been completely solved.  It is felt that the best
material available should be obtained and tried out.

       6.         This report contains very little information
on facilities at Dutch Harbor for submarines.  A complete report
on this is expected from Commander Submarine Division Forty-One
on his return from that area, in the S-34, in the near future.

                                        R. H. ENGLISH.

Copy to:
       CSD 41
       S-23
       S-18

                                        ENCLOSURE (C)
```

1st copy

U.S.S. S-23
SUBMARINE DIVISION FORTY-ONE

SS128/A16-3

July 10, 1942

Serial (02)

~~CONFIDENTIAL~~ DECLASSIFIED

From: The Commanding Officer.
To :   The Commander Submarines, Pacific Fleet.

Subject: U.S.S. S-23 Second War Patrol, Alaskan Area, May 20th-July 4th.

Reference: (a) ComSubPac Conf. Ltr. S-/2.

1.   This vessel left San Diego, California on Wednesday, May 20th in company with S-18, S-27 and S-28 escorted by the ARGONNE with secret verbal orders to proceed to this area by way of the Twelfth and thirteenth Naval District. The only event of note about the start of the cruise was that the Executive Officer had been sent to the hospital with measles, nine days before leaving. This left but four officers. Off the Farallons the U.S.S. ARGONNE relieved the ADMIRAL on escort [illegible] continue on to the Puget Sound area. On May 24th arrived Port Angeles at 0100 with S-1 and S-28, ARGONNE and S-27 going on to Seattle. At 1400 the next day departed for this area with ARGONNE, S-18 and S-28.

2.   The voyage up was without incident until May 30th when area assignments were received by dispatch for Commander Submarine Division FORTY-ONE with instructions to proceed direct. The direct route to this vessels area was through Akutan Pass then directly east past Dutch Harbor. We planned to proceed this way leaving the ARGONNE at Dutch Harbor. At 0900 June 1st S-27 left the formation to proceed direct to patrol station. At 1500 June 2nd S-18 left formation to proceed to patrol station. At 1700 ARGONNE with S-23 about two miles astern stood through Akutan Pass to the westward bucking a thirty knot wind and with an estimated five knot current. At 1730 a ship was sighted dead ahead by the ARGONNE on parallel and opposite course which proved to be a Russian freighter.

3.   The combination of wind and current in Akutan Pass is described as dangerous by the Sailing Directions, with heavy rip tides and twenty foot waves. We were prepared to take a few over the bridge but not at the rate of five every thirty seconds and that was how fast they came. The waves were about thirty feet high but the unusual thing about them was the short distance from crest to crest which was only about 150 feet.

DECLASSIFIED

By OP [illegible] Date 6/4/12

ENCLOSURE (C)

-1-

FILMED
87578

<u>CONFIDENTIAL</u>

Subject: U.S.S. S-33 - Report of Second War Patrol.

- -

4.   The bridge was flooded solid five times within a
minute. We dove immediately with the control room bilges
flooded. In the rescas on the bridge the Officer of the Deck
Lieutenant (jg) P.E. KLETT was injured by being thrown against
the periscope shears and suffered five broken ribs, the
Quartermaster First Class, MILLER, S.D., received contusions
of the face and a sprained right arm. Four galley smoke bombs
were fired in the next half hour to inform the KLETT who we
were doing much better below than above. We surfaced and proceeded to Dutch Harbor after which two cheers of green water to
the diesel platform.

5.   In view of the fact that we had an injured officer
and men aboard and were right off Dutch Harbor it was necessary
to hospitalize them before proceeding to patrol station. We
stood into Dutch Harbor to, the other unexpected arrival in
the following order: U.S. Army Transport WILLARD, S-33, U.S.S.
KLETT at about 1000 yard distance. For thirty minutes we gave
our call to the Army signal post as the entrance in attempted
to tell them we had two surgeon hospital cases aboard and requested that an Army or ambulance at the dock. All attempts at
communication were futile, this we all came to a quick stop when
a shell splashed about 400 yards ahead of us. With this they
sent "Heave to for inspection". A plane then circled us and we
received our second message "O.... told us in. We proceeded to
the dock at Dutch Harbor to get fuel and stores.

6.   The Commanding Officer called on the Commandant
Naval Air Station, Dutch Harbor and informed him they were
now down to three officers, the two new ensigns (one came to his
aboard, the other two) and himself. I learned in that that my
Executive Officer had been leaving battle on the S-7. Our
bridge force consisted of one Quartermaster Second Class and one
striker. At this time Ensign CROSBY MUTH also reported to
Naval Air Station Dutch Harbor from the U.S.S. ARGONAUT to the
U.S.S. S-23 and he was temporarily assigned to us.

7.   We planned to leave Dutch Harbor before noon next
day for patrol station and take the injured officer and men
along if at all possible. The Japs made a raid at 0550 so
that cancelled this arrangement. After the first raid we stood
out, and arrived in assigned patrol area at 2100 the same day.
Nothing was sighted in the area except friendly planes and on
June 11th orders were received to proceed Dutch Harbor for
fuel and stores and proceed to new patrol area southeast of
Attu. We arrived at Dutch Harbor at 0400 June 12th and left at
1500 the same day. We learned at this time that the Japs had
Kiska and Attu.

-2-

INKLOWN (C)

<u>CONFIDENTIAL</u>

Subject: U.S.S. S-23 - Report of Second War Patrol.

- -

8.   On June 13th at 1020 we dove when a mast was sighted on the horizon, it proved to be one of our own SS boats on patrol so we continued past, surfaced and proceeded on our way. At 1630 we had another mast sighted and we went [through] the procedure; this time it was the U.S.S. [illegible], which disappeared in a fog to the northward.

9.   We made a landfall on the east coast of Agattu Island at 1200 June 17th [illegible] from Cape Wpala Island by dead reckoning as it was overcast and a strong southeast wind was blowing all the time. We came within six miles of the land which was clouded in fog and then turned northward to [illegible] the Semichi Islands. At 1500 sighted [illegible] Semichi Islands and changed course to 305° (t), to stand up to the east coast of Attu Island which was covered by fog. The wind was about 6 knots from the east and the visibility was steadily poorer [illegible] the fog being blown down from Attu. At 1635 sighted a large tanker on a point forward of the starboard bow on opposite course about 4500 yards range just coming out of the fog. We dove and came to 070 to intercept and found ourselves still over 3000 yards away and about a 120° starboard angle. At this time (1705) a look around revealed another just coming out of the fog and crossing our stern as about 1000 yards range with a 100° port angle on the bow, headed [illegible] [illegible] to dove. The captain of the [illegible] was [illegible] station about one mile astern of the tanker and [illegible] could not be seen when we dove. We swung left to course 000° true for a shot but [illegible] and just made the course and the first [illegible]. At 1710 and fired two torpedoes at a range of about 1000 yards. We went to 100 feet to reload and the destroyer dropped three times as he passed down our port side so little was lost on going. The torpedoes were heard to run but no hits on [illegible]. Going down the range due to the north and our haze. At 1770 we surfaced for a look after reloading and saw it was still fog so we followed the track of the targets to the southeast and about ten miles southwest of the island the visibility was somewhat better but not over three miles.

10.   The patrol was continued on north and south courses that night and the next morning it was decided to investigate Sarana Bay on the northeast end of Attu Island where it was surmised the tanker and the destroyer had come from. Reconnaissance of Sarana Bay could not be made until Friday June 19th as fog continued heavy for 36 hours. From 1900 to 2200 June 19th made submerged reconnaissance Sarana Bay but saw nothing so stood down to northeast corner of area to meet anything coming back.

                                        [illegible] (C)

                    - 3 -

CONFIDENTIAL

Subject: U.S.S. S-23 - Report of Second War Patrol.
- -

On Saturday June 20th at 1000 sighted twin float monoplane
southeast similar to model Nakajima 93 and dove proceeding in
direction from which he came, plane continued on to west, in
about one hour picked up masts of large AP heading directly
for us range about 14,000 yards, we closed for attack but the
second look showed a 150° starboard angle and the target disappeared to the southwest. We attempted to surface and chase
but the plane reappeared to keep us down till dusk. Investigation the next day to the southwest and reconnaissance of the
south coast of Agattu Island showed nothing in sight, the
patrol was continued in the southwest corner of the area but
no targets appeared and there was no sight of the plane.

11.   On June 22nd decided to return to northeast
corner of area and saw a destroyer patrolling about three miles
east of McDonald dove at 1800 and the masts of AP could also
be seen inside. We stood in to attack but the fog came in
heavy so we patrolled to the eastward about five miles for the
next two days waiting for clear weather. In the meantime we
were set to the eastward about twenty miles so decided to surface when it cleared and stand West until a landfall could be
made. At 0915 June 25th while on the surface southeast of
the island a plane Nakajima 93 dove at us from quite close
behind a cloud but did not drop anything. We submerged and a
few hours later the destroyer was picked up on the starboard
beam about 4000 yards on opposite course. We could not attack,
and he disappeared in the haze to the northward.

12.   From June 25th to the time of leaving station
0000 July 1st the visibility was never more than four miles
for sixty percent of the time and for twenty percent of the
time it was not over 1000 yards. Needless to say no further
contacts or landfalls were made and the area was vacated to
the eastward for one day in a dense fog. On July 2nd and 3rd
clear weather was had for the first time in eleven days and it
was possible to get sun sights. We arrived at Dutch Harbor
at 0530 July 4th after being underway on forty seven consecutive days.

13.   The Charts for this area are unreliable and
the hydrographic information is meager. It is felt that more
than the usual percentage of fog was encountered. No major
defects were experienced but a cracked cell in the after battery had to be jumped out (#63). It will be replaced when

- 4 -   ENCLOSURE (C)

<u>CONFIDENTIAL</u>

Subject: U.S.S. S-23 - Report of Second War Patrol.
- -

a new element and jar is procured at an available tender or
base. The health of the crew and habitability of the boat was
excellent. The sound conditions were poor, the only target
that was heard was the destroyer we attacked after going to
200 feet. In the rough water encountered in this area a
topside mounted sound head is practically useless at periscope
depth. The miles steamed was 5850 and fuel expended 37,550
gallons. The factors of endurance remaining when recalled
to Dutch Harbor were:

Torpedoes   Fuel   Provisions   Fresh Water   Personnel

   10.   12 days   6 days   unlimited   6 days.

- 5 -   ENCLOSURE (C)

Summary of Contacts U.S.S. S-23

Position	Target	Course	Speed	Angle on Bow	Own Course	True Bearing	Time	Range	Results
				Contact #1 June 17th					
S.W. of Semichi Is.	Tanker	115°	14	75S-120S	285°-070°	000°	1700-1710	4500-3000	could not fire
				Contact #2 June 17th					
S.W. of Semichi Is.	Destroyer	240°	14	15P-45P	070°-000°	020°	1710-1715	3000-1000	Fired two torpedoes 60° port track missed
				Contact #3 June 20th					
North of Agattu Is.	Plane	270°	150°		190°	150°	0900	6000	Similar to Nakajima 93
				Contact #4 June 20th					
North of Agattu Is.	Large AP	000° 250°	10°	10°S-170S	170°	190°	0944	14,00	Target changed course to S.W. and disappeared.
				Contact #5 June 22nd					
Off McDonald Bay	Patrolling Destroyer	185°	14	0°	100°	005°	1810-1820	8000-4000	Target reversed course and disappeared in fog

Two repeated attacks on contact #5 were terminated when the target was sighted at a range of 1000 yards coming out of fog headed directly for us. No echo ranging was used by target, and no sound contacts were made by us.

ENCLOSURE (G)

1st end

FF12-10/A16-3(5) SUBMARINES, PACIFIC FLEET   M1

Serial 01063   Care of Fleet Post Office,
                                    San Francisco, California,
                                    September 14, 1942.

COMSUBPAC PATROL REPORT NO. 65
U.S.S. S-23 - THIRD WAR PATROL.

CONFIDENTIAL DECLASSIFIED

From: The Commander Submarines, Pacific Fleet.
To :   Submarines, Pacific Fleet.

Subject: U.S.S. S-23 (SS128) - Report of Third War
            Patrol.

Enclosure: (A) Copy of Comtaskgroup 8.5 Conf ltr TG8.5/
                A16-3 Serial 017 of August 29, 1942.
            (B) Copy of subject war patrol.

    1.   The remarks of Commander Task Group 8.5 in para-
graphs 2 and 3 of enclosure (A) are concurred in. Submarines
must retain the initiative by remaining at periscope depth as
long as possible and unless this is done, many valuable enemy
targets will be permitted to escape.

                                    R. E. ENGLISH.

DISTRIBUTION
   (21CN-42)
List I, Case 2:
  Pl(5), SSs
Special:
  EN3(5); Comsublant (2);
  Comsubsowespac (2);
  Cominch (5).

E. R. SWINBURNE,
Flag Secretary.

FILED
87579

TG8.5/A16-3   August 29, 1942.

Serial 017

<u>CONFIDENTIAL</u>

From: The Commander Task Group Eight Point Five.
To :   The Commander Submarines, Pacific Fleet.

Subject: U.S.S. S-23 - Report of Third War Patrol.

Reference: (a) CO U.S.S. S-23 Confid. ltr. File SS128/
                 A16-3 Serial (03) dated August 18, 1942.

Enclosure: (A) Reference (a) with Enclosure (A) thereto.

    1.   The third War Patrol of the S-23 covered a period of thirty-four days, of which twenty-seven were spent in various patrol areas and on station on a patrol arc covering the bombardment of Kiska Harbor. Comment on previous patrol reports of S-class submarines in the Aleutian area, with respect to the need for fathometer, radar, and underwater sound equipment are applicable here.

    2.   The narrative, which written chronologically, does not follow the usual form of separating entries by dates, which is considered preferable.

    3.   The probability of hitting with Mark Ten torpedoes from the unfavorable firing position on August fifteen was slight. It is understood that the target did not appear to be following a zig zag plan. This fact, plus the type of ship, indicates that she was patrolling. It is possible that a better firing position might have been attained as a result of subsequent maneuvers of the target. While the lines resembled those of the Q-ship reported by the GUDGEON, that she was such a ship is questionable, in view of the fact that her guns were visibile.

    4.   The S-23 returned from patrol in excellent material condition.

                          Enclosure (A)

CONFIDENTIAL

U.S.S. S-23 - REPORT OF THIRD WAR PATROL.

PERIOD FROM JULY 15, 1943 to AUGUST 18, 1942.

AREA: ALASKAN.   OPERATION ORDER: COMTASKGROUP 8.5 OpORDER 5-42.

   1. NARRATIVE.

     1.   Left Dutch Harbor at 1800 William July 15, 1942 for patrol area in accordance with Commander Task Group 8.5 Operation Order 5-42 of July 15, 1942. Made several training dives enroute and at 0900Kray, July 17, entered our assigned area, ATU. SOUTH. Dove at 1100 and conducted submerged reconnaissance of southern coast of ATU. At 0200 Kray on July 18, received Commander Task Group 8.5 dispatch 181040 assigning new patrol station. Decided to spend one more day in ATU. SOUTH and then leave for new area. At 1100 on above date sighted a PBY on easterly course, distance about 10 miles. He apparently did not see us as he made no investigation.

     2.   At 1200 Kray, July 19, left the area. At 0750 Yoke, July 20, sighted an unidentified patrol type flying boat on our starboard quarter, headed toward us. Dove. At 0810 surfaced and sighted two unidentified planes ten miles to the southward on an easterly course. Remained on surface as these planes soon passed out of sight. Arrived on station at 0700 Yoke on July 21 and commenced surface patrol. During this and succeeding nine days on this station while waiting for BAKER DAY to take place, visibility conditions were exceedingly poor with fog prevailing continually. During this period, nothing was seen nor heard.

     3.   On July 30, received work that BAKER DAY had been deferred and assigned us the new patrol area of ATTU and ATTU . Arrived in this area at 1200 Yoke, July 31 and commenced a surface patrol with the low visibility continuing. At 1400 on August 1, made landfall on CAPE RAIKELL, ATTU. This was our first sight of land or fix of position since July 20. During the afternoon made submerged examination of ETIENNE B.Y. Results negative. On August 3 we continued our submerged patrol of the bays and harbors along the west and southwestern coast of ATTU. Again nothing was seen. At 0345 Yoke on August 6, received TRIGGER'S contact report of one auxiliary and two destroyers north of RED HEAD on course 270°T. We headed north on possibility of intercepting although we were too far south in our area to give us much hope of accomplishing this. At 1600 gave up and changed course to the southeast to return the limits of our area as assigned for BAKER DAY.

     4.   After the Attack on KISKA by our surface forces had taken place we were assigned Area ATTU and we entered this area at 0600 Yoke, August 9. At 1420 Yoke on this date while making a submerged patrol along the northern coast of the SEMICHI ISLANDS we sighted the masts of three ships about 6 miles to the north of

-1-   ENCLOSURE (B)

CONFIDENTIAL

Subject: U.S.S. S-23 - Report of Third War Patrol.
- -

us. Ships appeared to be on an easterly course with a fairly large angle on the bow. We changed course to 070°T to attempt to close the range. The ships passed out of sight before they could be definitely identified but believed them to be one destroyer and two auxiliaries. At 1600 surfaced and sent contact report.

5.   At 0410 Yoke, August 11, received orders to patrol sector between bearings of 247°T from CAPE WRANGELL in order to intercept enemy vessels making landfall on or taking departure from ATTU. Proceeded to this area and commenced surface patrol along initial great circle course between ATTU and HOKOLUSHIRU. On August 13 returned to north coast of ATTU to search for destroyers in CHICAGOF HARBOR and HOLTZ BAY in accordance with Commander Task Group 8.5 dispatch 130251. Made submerged approach to CHICAGOF HARBOR. There was no indication of enemy vessels in the outer portion of the harbor. Fog prevented our seeing the inner end of the harbor but do not believe there were any ships there. Was unable to investigate HOLTZ BAY as fog was closing in. Low visibility on August 14 prevented further investigation of these harbors.

6.   At dark August 14 departed area enroute Dutch Harbor in accordance with Commander Task Group 8.5 dispatch 110908. At 0830 Yoke, August 15, when about 60 miles bearing 335° from KISKA sighted masts of a vessel bearing 190°T distance ten miles. Dove and commenced approach. Identified ship as a patrol vessel of approximately 1000 tons, similar to the O-ship illustrated in GUDGEON second war patrol report. Was unable to close target sufficiently to obtain a very favorable firing range but at 0925 fired tubes #3 and #4 at a range of 2500 yards with a 130° starboard track. Both shots missed and it is believed they passed ahead. After firing, target appeared to be turning toward us and we went to 200 feet. Did not hear any pinging and the JK was unable to pick up sound of screws. At 0942 came up to periscope depth. The ship was then standing away to the northwest. Surfaced when the ship was out of sight and continued to DUTCH HARBOR. Sighted several PBY's and Army Bombers during next two days enroute to port but nothing further of interest occurred. At 0800 William August 18 arrived DUTCH HARBOR.

8. WEATHER

    Visibility was extremely poor during the entire patrol and particularly during the period from July 19 to July 30 while on station west of KISKA. During those 10 days, visibility was less than five miles 95 percent of the time, and less than 1000 yards 75 percent of the time. On the exceptional days which were not foggy, visibility was very good. Seas and winds were moderate during the patrol.

CONFIDENTIAL

Subject: U.S.S. S-23 - REPORT OF THIRD WAR PATROL.
- -

3.   TIDAL INFORMATION.

        No comment.

4.   NAVIGATIONAL AIDS.

        None. Charts of the ATTU - AGATTU area are incomplete
and unreliable.

5.   DESCRIPTION OF ENEMY VESSELS SIGHTED.

Contact No.	Date	Time	Description	Position	Course	Speed
1	8/9/42	1420	2 Auxiliaries 1 Yoko Destroyer.Unable to further ident-ify due to great range.	15 Miles north of SEMICH IS. Lat.53°-01N. Long.174°-00E.	110°	12 kts.
2	8/14/42	0830	1 Small patrol Yoko vessel similar to A-ship.Disp 1000 tons.	80 miles,335°T from KISKA.Lat. 53°-25N.Long. 176°-48'E.	Zigzagging.Base course about 315°T	10 kts.

6.   DESCRIPTION OF AIRCRAFT SIGHTED.

Date	Time	Description	Position	Course	Altitude
7/18/42	1100 Xray	1 Navy PBY	Lat. 51°44'N Long.175°20'W	090°	1000 feet.
7/20/42	0750 Yoko	1 Patrol Type Flying Boat Unidentified.	Lat. 50°31'N Long.179°52'W	315°	500 feet.
7/20/42	0810 Yoko	2 Patrol Type Flying Boats Unidentified.	Lat. 50°30'N Long.179°54'W	090°	1500 feet.
8/16/42 17		Several PBY's and Army Bombers on patrol out of DUTCH HARBOR.			

7.   SUMMARY OF SUBMARINE ATTACKS.

Attack No.	Torps. Fired	Est. Range	Fir. Int.	Point of aim	Track angle	Dep Set	Est. Drt.	Est. Spd.	Torpedo Perform
1	2	2500 Yards	11 secs.	M.O.T.	130S	10'	13'	10	Normal

- 3 -

<u>ENCLOSURE (B)</u>

CONFIDENTIAL

Subject: U.S.S. S-23 - REPORT OF THIRD WAR PATROL.
- -

RESULTS: Both torpedoes missed. It is believed that they
passed ahead of the target.

8.   ENEMY A/S MEASURES.

None encountered.

9.   MAJOR DEFECTS EXPERIENCED.

None.

10.   RADIO RECEPTION.

1. Radio reception was generally good. High noise level on
NPM Fox low frequency made it necessary to shift to high frequency
on several occasions. Submerged loop is defective and we were unable to receive when submerged.

2.   Three messages were sent, all receipted for by NPR. All of
Commander Task Group 8.5 dispatches were received.

11.   SOUND CONDITIONS AND DENSITY LAYERS.

Sound conditions did not appear to be favorable. We were unable to pick up screws of vessels in either contacts made and they
did not appear to make sound contact with us.

12.   HEALTH AND HABITABILITY.

Health of the crew was excellent. Habitability of the boat
was good due to the moderate seas.

13.   MILES STEAMED ENROUTE TO AND FROM STATION.

Fifteen hundred miles were steamed enroute to and from patrol
areas.

14.   FUEL OIL EXPENDED.

22,600 gallons.

15.   FACTORS OF ENDURANCE REMAINING.

Torpedoes	Fuel	Provisions	Fresh Water	Personnel
10	5120 gals.	0 days	Unlimited	0 days

16.   FACTOR OF ENDURANCE TERMINATING PATROL.
Orders to return to port.

17.   REMARKS.
None.

- 4 -   ENCLOSURE (B)

1st copy

FF12-10/A16-3(5) SUBMARINE FORCE, PACIFIC FLEET   1d

Serial 01247   Care of Fleet Post Office,
                                        San Francisco, California,
                                        31 October 1942

CONFIDENTIAL

COMSUBPAC PATROL REPORT NO. 82
U.S.S. S-23 - FOURTH WAR PATROL.

From: The Commander Submarine Force, Pacific Fleet.
To :   Submarine Force, Pacific Fleet.

Subject: U.S.S. S-23 (SS128) - Report of Fourth War
          Patrol.

Enclosure: (A) ComTaskGroup 8.5 Conf. ltr. TG8.5/A16-3
                Serial (027) of September 21, 1942.
           (B) Subject War Patrol.

     1.   Enclosures (A) and (B) are forwarded for in-
formation.

                                        R. H. ENGLISH.

DISTRIBUTION
   (35CM-42)
List III: SSs.
Special:
   P1(5), EN3(5), Z1(5)
   Comsublant (2),
   Comsubsowespac (2)

E. R. SWINBURNE,
Flag Secretary.

TG8.5/AJ8-3
Serial (027)

Naval Operating Base,
Dutch Harbor, Alaska,
September 21, 1942.

CONFIDENTIAL

From: The Commander Task Group Eight Point Five.
To: The Commander Submarines, Pacific Fleet.

Subject: U.S.S. S-23 – Report of Fourth War Patrol.

1.   This, the fourth War Patrol of the U.S.S. S-23, covered a period of twenty-four days. Recall from patrol was dictated by her scheduled departure on September 20 for San Diego for upkeep and Sound School services.

2.   The area to which the S-23 was assigned during this patrol was prescribed for protective scouting in connection with an amphibious operation. No contacts with the enemy were had.

3.   Considering the length of time the S-23 has operated on war patrols from an advanced base, her material condition is considered excellent.

ENCLOSURE (A)

<u>CONFIDENTIAL</u>

Subject: U.S.S. S-23 — REPORT OF FOURTH WAR PATROL.
             PERIOD FROM AUGUST 26 TO SEPTEMBER 18, 1942.

- -

1. <u>NARRATIVE</u>

August 26   0947(W) Departed Submarine Base, Dutch Harbor,
            Alaska for patrol Area ____ in accordance with
            Commander Task Group 8.5 Mailgram of August 26,
            1942. 1905(X) Made trim dive. 1925(X) Surfaced.

August 28   0636.(X) Sighted U.S. Army B-17 on easterly course.
            Submerged. 0730(X) Surfaced. 1159(X) Sighted
            unidentified plane on port quarter. Submerged.
            1245(X) Surfaced. 2057(Y) Entered assigned area.

August 29 - September 13 - Patrolled in assigned area on
            various courses, mostly on surface, diving in
            early morning and when necessary to avoid friend-
            ly planes on routine search flights; acting as
            "protective scout" for occupation of Adak Island
            by Army Forces. Surfaced in late mornings.
            Area was 30 miles X 30 miles in size.

September 14 - 16 - Conducted patrol in area submerged dur-
            ing daylight after receipt of dispatch from Com-
            mander Task Group 8.5 to conduct patrol submerged
            in clear weather. 1900(Y) Left area to return to
            Dutch Harbor in accordance with Commander Task
            Group 8.5 dispatch 141011.

September 17 - 18 - Enroute from Area ____ to Dutch Harbor.
            September 18, 1930(W) entered Dutch Harbor.

2. Weather -

            Heavy seas and a force 7-9 Southerly wind were
            encountered on September 4 - 5 and 15 - 16. The
            rest of the time the sea was moderate, visibility
            good, weather temperate, although the sky was
            overcast about 70 per cent of the time. Of the
            eight months this vessel has operated in the
            Alaskan Area the period covered by this patrol
            was the most favorable yet encountered for all
            types of operation.

  3. Tidal Information -
            No comment.

  4. Navigational Aids -
            No comment.

  5. Description of Enemy Vessels sighted -
            None sighted.

                              -1-   ENCLOSURE "B"

<u>CONFIDENTIAL</u>

Subject: U.S.S. S-23 - Report of Fourth War Patrol.

- -

6. Description of all aircraft sighted.

<u>Date</u>	<u>Time</u>	<u>Description</u>	<u>Position</u>	<u>Course</u>	<u>Altitude</u>
Aug. 28	0638(X)	U.S. Army Bomber B-17.	53-27.0N 174-34.5W	090	3000 Ft.
Aug. 28	1200(X)	U.S. Navy PBY	53-22.0N 176-08.0W	000	1000 ft.
Aug. 30	0700(Y)	U.S. Army Bomber B-17	53-26.0N 178-27.0W	270	8000 ft.
Sept. 9	1017(Y)	U.S. Navy SBC*	53-07.0N 177-59.4W	045	1000 ft.
Sept.11	1230(Y)	Unidentified	52-56.0N 178-35.0W	270	1500 ft.
Sept.12	0706(Y)	Unidentified	53-20.0N 178-40.0W	345	500 ft.
Sept.13	1032(Y)	U.S. Navy PBY	53-07.0N 177-56.0W	090	500 ft.
Sept.14	1330(Y)	U.S. Navy Kingfisher*	53-04.0N 178.35.0W	270	1500 ft.
Sept.18	Various	Various Army and Navy Types	Routine Search Patrols of Umnak and Unalaska Island.	Various	Various

* Not clearly identified -

7. Summary of Submarine Attacks.
   None made.

8. Enemy A/S Measures.
   None encountered.

9. Major defects experienced.
   None.

10.Radio Reception.
   Reception from NPM and NPG was good. The high frequency had
   a rather high noise level but was readable. This vessel sent
   one message to NPR with no difficulty on 8290. Last message
   received from Commander Task Group 8.5 - Virega Island.

11. Sound conditions and density layers.
   No comment - no contacts made.

12. <u>Health and Habitability.</u>
   Health of crew was excellent. Habitability was excellent
   within limitations inherent in S-types submarine.

13. <u>Miles steamed enroute to and from station.</u>
   900 miles.

14. <u>Fuel oil expended.</u>
   12750 gallons.

-2-   ENCLOSURE "B"

CONFIDENTIAL

Subject: U.S.S. S-23 - REPORT OF FOURTH WAR PATROL.

15. Factors of endurance remaining:

Torpedoes	Fuel	Provisions	Fresh Water	Personnel
12	15000 gallons	18 days	Unlimited	10 days

16. Factor of endurance ending patrol.
        Orders of Commander Task Group 8.5.

17. Remarks.
        None.

-3-   ENCLOSURE "B".

1st Copy

Reg. No. 85 8 2
R.S. No. 3 033

FF12-10/A16-3
TB5-41

Serial 0177

SUBMARINE FORCE, PACIFIC FLEET

Care of Fleet Post Office;
San Francisco, California,
February 9, 1943.

CONFIDENTIAL ~~DECLASSIFIED~~

CONSUBPAC PATROL REPORT NO. 135
U.S.S. S-23 - FIFTH WAR PATROL.

From: The Commander Submarine Force, Pacific Fleet.
To :   Submarine Force, Pacific Fleet.

Subject: U.S.S. S-23 (SS128) - Report of Fifth War Patrol.

Enclosure: (A) Copy of Subject War Patrol.
           (B) Copy of ComTaskGroup 8.5 Conf ltr
               TG8.5/A16-3 Serial 03 of Jan. 9, 1943.

    1.   No remarks.

                              J.W. BROWN, JR.,
                              Acting.

DISTRIBUTION
    (1M-43)
List III: SS.
Special:
    P1(5), EM3(5), 71(5),
    ComSublant (2), X3(1),
    Comsubsowespac (2);
    Subschool N.J. (2),
    CTF 42 (2).

E.R. SWINBURNE,
Flag Secretary.

46465 FILMED

U.S.S. S-23 - REPORT OF FIFTH WAR PATROL PERIOD FROM DECEMBER 17, 1942, TO JANUARY 6, 1943.

OPERATION ORDER - COMTASKGROUP 8.5 NO. 39-42.

PROLOGUE

Departed San Diego, California, November 21 after 3 weeks overhaul period in which major accomplishments were installation of NJ-3 type fathometer, SJ Radar, Kleinschmidt type still, and replacement of starboard main motor armature. Arrived at Dutch Harbor Submarine Base on December 7, 1942. Went into upkeep status for repair of two grounded field coils in starboard main motor and repair to radar equipment. Departed Dutch Harbor at 1543(W), December 17, 1942 for area _______ in accordance with Commander Task Group 8.5 Operation Order 39-42. Two grounded field coils in starboard motor still out of commission. SJ radar working satisfactorily. Model LM-8, A.C. operated, frequency meter installed by Dutch Harbor, Submarine Base. No training period.

1. NARRATIVE.

December 17, 1942.
1800(W) Took departure from Priest Rock set course for assigned area.

December 18, 1942.
0400(W) Contact on radar. Range 4000 yards. Contact appeared to be moving on westerly course at high speed as radar soon lost contact at 7000 yards. Officer of Deck believed he saw shadow in direction of contact but not sure. Captain saw nothing.

December 18-21, 1942.
Uneventful - daily dives at morning and evening twilight.
December 21, 1942 - 1200(Y) - Entered assigned area.
December 22, 1942.
0830(Y) Made landfall on western end of Attu Island.

December 22-23, 1942.
Too rough for inshore periscope patrol; running on generally northeast - southwest line as direction of seas dictate. 2325(Y) Received Commander Task Group 8.5 Egg Harbor assigned vessel patrol station off Paramushiro.

December 24, 1942.
0700(Y) Took departure from Cape Wrangel, Attu Island for Horomushiro via rhumb line. 0840(Y) crossed international date line but did not change date. Dutch Harbor date will be used throughout patrol. Un-

- 1 -   ENCLOSURE (1)

<u>CONFIDENTIAL</u>

Subject: U.S.S. S-23 - Report of Fifth War Patrol.
- -

December 24, 1942. (Cont'd)
        usually excellent weather during day and night.

December 25, 1942.
        Made routine dives; held battle surface and fired
        two rounds from deck gun.

December 26, 1942.
1700(L) Upon attempting to make routine evening dive, dis-
        covered that stern plane operating gear outside hull
        apparently broken. Boat could be submerged only with
        great difficulty and with no depth control as stern
        planes were apparently jammed on hard rise. 1800(L)
        Decided to return to base and set course for Point __.
        Did not send message to Commander Task Group 8.5 at
        this time as we were only 200 miles from Paramushiro
        and hence, afraid of enemy D/F.

December 27, 1942.
2100(L) Sent Attu Island to Commander Task Group 8.5 in-
        forming him of our predicament, and estimated time
        arrival 200 mile circle from Point __. Making stand-
        ard speed on both engines, but drag of stern planes
        is noticeable, especially on port. Port engine is
        running at full throttle with no float in order to
        make required turns. Starboard engine can still
        carry customary float, but load on both is severe.

December 28, 1942.
1100(L) Decided to stop port shaft and run starboard shaft
        at 305 turns by running starboard engine at throttle
        setting for 260 turns and making difference by using
        starboard motor. Port engine is in use charging
        batteries to compensate for increased load. This
        procedure was resorted to in order to relieve load
        on engines and to prevent fouling of port shaft
        which is apparently the one interfered with most by
        the stern planes.

December 30, 1942.
1030(Y) Sighted PBY on opposite and parallel course. Appar-
        ently did not see us. 1200(Y) Sighted what appeared
        to be same plane returning to base.

                    - 2 -   ENCLOSURE (A)

<u>CONFIDENTIAL</u>

Subject: U.S.S. S-23 - Report of Fifth War Patrol.
- -

December 31, 1942.
1145(Y) Sighted PBY heading for us. Attempted exchange of
         recognition signals but ours did not jibe with what
         he was using. It looked as if he was using the signal
         for the next day. Plane circled us and then departed
         on westerly course. Plane sighted returning to base
         about one hour later.

January 4-5, 1942.
         Very cold weather with much snow, ice, and wind.
         Afternoon of 5th lost 3 of 4 sections of radio
         antennae because weight of ice on them became too
         great. Not practical to dive to rid topside of ice
         because of stern planes.

January 6, 1942.
1030(W) Entered Dutch Harbor, Alaska.

II. <u>WEATHER</u>.

     The weather for the most part was excellent, considering the
area of operations. Only on about two days was the sea rough
enough to make the course steered a matter of concern, and at no
time was it rough enough to prevent steering a selected course.
However, maintainance of periscope depth would have been impossible except for about 3 days.

     Visibility was good to excellent on the way to patrol station
around Attu, and to the West. On the return trip the customary
winter rain and snow squalls were encountered during the last
half.

     Temperature was about the expected average; the coldest tem-
perature encountered being 24°F one day out of Dutch Harbor on
the return trip.

     In general the weather was a pleasurable contrast to that
which this boat had come to expect from previous experience during the winter months in this area.

III. <u>TIDAL INFORMATION</u>.

     At end of 24 hour run to westward after taking depature from
Cape Wrangel, Attu Island for Horomushiro a drift of 1.0 knots
and a set of 076° true was experienced.

                              - 3 -   ENCLOSURE (A)

CONFIDENTIAL

Subject: U.S.S. S-23 - Report of Fifth War Patrol. - - - - - - - - -

IV. NAVIGATIONAL AIDS.

No comment.

V. CONTACTS

None made.

VI. AIRCRAFT SIGHTED.

No.	Time Date	Lat.Long.	Type	Est. Range	Alt.	Course	Remarks
1	1030Y	50-15.0N 176-20.0E	PBY	12 mi.	8000 ft	270	Apparently did not see us.
2	1200Y	50-18.0N 176-25.0E	PBY	12 mi.	8000 ft	090	Probably plane above returning.
3	1145Y	50-20.0N 179-50.5W	PBY	--	1000 ft	180	Circled and exchanged recognition signals.

VII. Summary of Submarine Attacks Made.

None Made.

VIII. Enemy A/S Measures.

None encountered.

IX. Enemy Mine Sweeping.

None encountered.

X. Major defects experienced.

On December 26, while attempting to make routine dive stern plane operating gear external to the hull apparently broke, as no control of stern planes was possible. This casualty has also apparently damaged the port propellor. No investigation of this casualty is possible while at sea, so no further comment can be made.

XI. Radio Reception.

Radio reception of NPG was good as far west as Attu but grew progressively worse as the further west we went. East of Attu NPG could be copied on 19.6 Kcs, 7065 Kcs, and 14150 during the day and on 19.6 Kcs and 14150 Kcs at night. West of Attu more and more time had to be spent on 14150 Kcs until all copying day and

<u>CONFIDENTIAL</u>

Subject: U.S.S. S-23 - Report of Fifth War Patrol.

- -

night was done on 14150 Kcs. No difficulty was encountered in working Dutch Harbor on 4235 Kcs; our first message, sent when we were about 1200 miles from Dutch Harbor being received at strength two without use of full transmitting power. Last message sent - Cove Bay. Last message received - Naha Bay.

XII.   <u>Sound Conditions and Density Layers.</u>

 No comment.

XIII.   <u>Health and Habitability.</u>

 Health was excellent. One officer had two teeth broken and one knocked loose when a wave threw him against the spray shield on the bridge.
 Habitability was good, consistent with the inherent limitations of S-type submarines, because of the comparatively mild weather.

XIV.   <u>Miles Steamed.</u>

 To first area assigned - 662 miles. From furthest westward point - 1356 miles.

XV.   <u>Fuel Expended.</u>

 18,473 Gallons.

XVI.   <u>Factors of endurance remaining.</u>

<u>Torpedoes</u>	<u>Fuel</u>	<u>Provisions</u>	<u>Fresh Water</u>	<u>Personnel</u>
12	9177	10 days	Unlimited	11

XVII.   <u>Reason for ending patrol.</u>
Material casualty (stern planes).

XVIII. Remarks.

 While in San Diego, an upper conning tower hatch with a higher combing was installed in place of the old one. This has proved of great value as it has prevented a considerable amount of water from flooding into the control room, especially when running before the seas. As a result the boat is not so hampered in choice of courses in moderately rough weather by fear of being pooped. However, this type of hatch makes clearing of the bridge a little more awkward. It is believed, though, that operation of the SJ Radar, which is installed in the conning tower would be severely hampered in the weather encountered in this

- 5 - ENCLOSURE (A)

CONFIDENTIAL

Subject: U.S.S. S-23 - Report of Fifth War Patrol.
- -

area without this type of hatch to prevent the great amount of
water which this boat customarily previously took aboard from
flooding into the control room.

The question of adequate clothing for the bridge watch is
still not solved. The question has two problems; keeping warm
and keeping dry. There exists at present a navy clothing which
will give sufficient warmth without being so bulky as to hamper
movement and complicate the stowage problem while at sea. The
new issue of rubberized trousers and parkas seem to be fairly
adequate in keeping the body dry but it is somewhat of a problem
to put them over all the clothes one must wear to keep warm.
The ideal garment would be a fleece-lined waterproof parka and
trousers.

The present standard issue of blue jungle cloth foul
weather clothing is not adequate for sea duty in this climate.
The aviation personnel are issued a fleece lined version of
this clothing. It is recommended that this type of clothing be
made available to submarines.

The most serious problems in regard to foul weather
clothing, however, in order of urgency are gloves and boots.
The present standard issue cold weather glove is absolutely useless for submarines as one can not keep his hands dry. Some
sort of fur lined waterproof gloves are very urgently needed.
This boat has tried several types of rubberized gloves and mittens
obtained on open purchase but they have not proven adequate to
the demands made upon them. At present this boat is experimenting
with using the standard stock lineman's gloves over a couple
of pair of woolen mittens. While this gear, without doubt,
keeps the hands dry, it is clumsy, cold, and uses very high grade
rubber for a task which should be performed by inferior stuff.

The present issue of fabric top overshoes should be replaced by a short rubber boot. The overshoes are neither warm
enough or dry enough.

- 6 -   ENCLOSURE (A)

TG8.5/A16-3
Serial 03

January 9, 1943.

<u>CONFIDENTIAL</u>

From: The Commander Task Group Eight Point Five
    (Commander Submarine Squadron Forty-Five).
To : The Commander Submarine Force, Pacific Fleet.

Subject: U.S.S. S-23 - Fifth War Patrol.

1. Unfortunately this patrol was cut short by a casualty to the stern planes. This is the second boat to return from patrol with stern plane trouble. On this vessel the casualty was caused by the pin connecting the stern plane yoke connecting rod to the port plane either sheering or dropping out. This allowed the planes to swing free and eventually upset and break the stop. The planes then fouled and wrecked both propellers. No dry dock or marine railway being available at this base the stern planes were repaired and propellers renewed by trimming down and using a floating and mobile crane for additional lift. The fouling of the rudder by the stern planes caused excessive wear, to the point of chewing up, of the gear train in the steering gear box. The gear chain from the S-35, which was returning to the navy yard, was exchanged to insure reliability of steering while S-23 is on patrol.

2. Although no contacts were made on this patrol it was not without value as it demonstrated that the alterations being made to S-class submarines are enhancing their military value. The combing installed with the spider type conning tower hatch has reduced the amount of green water taken into the control room, which makes the boats more seaworthy and habitable and should reduce some of the electrical troubles caused thereby. The SJ radar proved itself very rugged and remained in operation without casualty during the entire patrol in spite of its exposed location in the conning tower.

3. Winter clothing for submarines has been made the subject of a special report by this command. The three factors of (1) bulkiness, (2) dryness, and (3) warmth seem to be a combination that can not be coordinated to produce a satisfactory garment.

Copy to:
 Comtaskforce 8
 Consubdiv 41.

          ENCLOSURE (B)

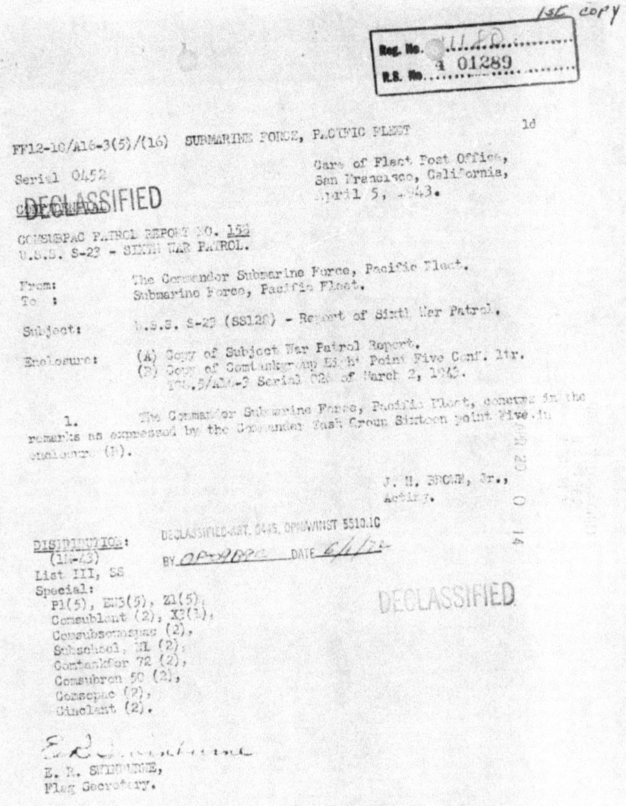

Reg. No. ....
R.S. No. A 01289

1st COPY

FF12-10/A16-3(5)/(16)   SUBMARINE FORCE, PACIFIC FLEET   ld

Serial 0452   Care of Fleet Post Office,
                                   San Francisco, California,
CONFIDENTIAL   April 5, 1943.
DECLASSIFIED

COMSUBPAC PATROL REPORT NO. 155
U.S.S. S-23 - SIXTH WAR PATROL.

From: The Commander Submarine Force, Pacific Fleet.
To :   Submarine Force, Pacific Fleet.

Subject: U.S.S. S-23 (SS128) - Report of Sixth War Patrol.

Enclosure: (A) Copy of Subject War Patrol Report.
             (B) Copy of ComTaskGroup Eight Point Five Conf. ltr.
                 FF6.5/A16-3 Serial 028 of March 2, 1943.

     1.   The Commander Submarine Force, Pacific Fleet, concurs in the
remarks as expressed by the Commander Task Group Sixteen point Five in
enclosure (B).

                                        J. H. BROWN, Jr.,
                                        Acting.

DISTRIBUTION: DECLASSIFIED-ART. 0445, OPNAVINST 5510.1C
   (1M-43)   BY OP-09BC   DATE 6/1/72
List III, SS
Special:
   P1(5), EN3(5), Z1(5),
   Consublant (2), X3(1),
   Consubsorpspac (2),
   Subschool, NL (2),
   Comtankfor 72 (2),
   Comsubron 50 (2),
   Comsopac (2),
   Cinclant (2).

E. R. SWINBURNE,
Flag Secretary.

48148 FILMED

TG8.5/A16-3

Serial 026   Ps

CONFIDENTIAL   March 2, 1943.

From: The Commander Task Group Eight point five,
             (Commander Submarine Squadron Forty-Five).
To :   The Commander Submarine Force, Pacific Fleet.

Subject: U.S.S. S-23 - Report of Sixth War Patrol.

Enclosure: (A) Subject Report.

    1.   The Sixth War Patrol of the U.S.S. S-23 covered a period of thirty (30) days, of which twenty-one (21) days were spent in patrol areas. The only contact was with the ship in CHICHAGOF HARBOR on February 2, which evidently followed the usual JAPANESE practice of leaving under cover of darkness. A close-in radar search should be conducted during darkness under these circumstances to insure interception. The Commanding Officer's decision to patrol on the surface in Area _______ is considered sound in that it increased his coverage of routes from the EMPIRE. The patrol was well conducted, the assigned areas being thoroughly covered.

    2.   The material condition of the S-23 was excellent, permitting the refit period to be reduced from fourteen to ten days. The morale of the crew was excellent, considering the lack of stimulation resulting from the absence of enemy contacts.

ENCLOSURE (B)

CONFIDENTIAL   Ps

Subject: U.S.S. S-23 - Report of Sixth War Patrol.
- -
                PERIOD FROM JANUARY 28, 1943, to Feb. 26, 1943.

AREA ________________

DPERATION ORDER - COMTASKGROUP 8.5 NO. 5-43.

PROLOGUE

        Arrived Submarine Base, Dutch Harbor, Alaska from patrol.
Base personnel assisted by Ships Force, gave routine overhaul
and refit with additional sailor stand - replaced lost pin in
stern plane outboard mechanism linkage, repaired broken mechanical stops on stern planes, and renewed all blades on port trim-
pellers. January 20, 1943 under way for Kodiak, Alaska, for dock-
ing to repair leak in forward trim tank. January 21, 1943 entered
drydock. January 22, 1943 left drydock, repairs not yet satisfactorily work accomplished. January 23, 1943 departed Kodiak,
Alaska for Dutch Harbor, Alaska. January 26, 1943 arrived at Submarine Base, Dutch Harbor, Alaska. January 28, 1943 left Dutch
Harbor, Alaska for patrol in Area ________________ in accordance with
Commander Task Group 8.5 operation order 5-43. Have on board one
relief crew section. Partial training accomplished on trip to
and from Kodiak, Alaska.

II NARRATIVE

January 28, 1943.
    1100(W)   Under way from Dutch Harbor, Alaska for Area ______
              in accordance with Commander Task Group 8.5 Opera-
              tion Order 5-43. Rendezvoused with escort at har-
              bor entrance. During early afternoon held radar
              training runs with escort as target. 1500(W) Re-
              leased escort. 1630(W) Made trim dive. 1700(W)
              Surfaced.

January 29, 1943.
    1430(W)   Set clocks to plus 11 zone time. 1350(X) Sighted
              life raft of type carried by surface ships. Painted
              war color, contained oars, first aid kit, emergency
              rations and canteen but no identification. Posi-
              tion 53-42N 172-51W. Made routine morning and even-
              ing twilight dives.

January 30, 1943.
              Made routine morning and evening twilight dives.
              1430(X) Set clocks to plus 12 zone time.

                              ENCLOSURE (A)
                    - 1 -

<u>CONFIDENTIAL</u>   Ps

Subject: U.S.S. S-23 - Report of Sixth War Patrol.
- -

January 31, 1943.
          Made routine morning and evening twilight dives.
          0750(Y) While submerged heard noise over J.K. sound
          gear - all around dial - strong resemblance to ping-
          ing but not like usual pings - audible only when re-
          ceiver was tuned to 18 Kcs. Nothing in sight. Po-
          sition: 53-16N; 179-44W. 0815(Y) Surfaced. 0947(Y)
          Made quick dive upon sighting of 4 planes in for-
          mation on parallel course, distant about 8 miles.
          Planes too far for identification but were of small
          type with no floats. Apparently did not see us.
          1011(Y) Surfaced. 1425(Y) Sighted what appeared to
          be a PBY 10° on port bow, headed this way. Dove.
          1449(Y) Surfaced, nothing in sight.

February 1, 1943.
     1110(Y) Entered area ___________ . 1745(Y) Sighted Attu
          Island bearing 314°T distant 25 miles. Made routine
          dives. During night running on surface on a north-
          east - southwest course. Plan to approach Attu in
          early morning and make periscope patrol from Holtz
          Bay to Sarana Bay.

February 2, 1943.
     0435(Y) Sighted steady white light on beach in vicinity of
          Chichagof Harbor. 0645(Y) Sighted smoke in vicin-
          ity of Chichagof Harbor. 0745(Y) Dived. Low visi-
          bility prevented reconnaissance of Chichagof Harbor
          in morning so proceeded to Sarana Bay which proved
          negative of results. Returned to Chichagof Harbor.
          1420(Y) Saw that smoke sighted early in morning
          came from small steamer in inner harbor. Closest
          we could approach was about 4000 yards as harbor
          narrowed to approximately 500 yards at that point.
          Decided long range, small target, and heavy ground
          swells did not justify expenditure of a torpedo.
          Ship had two rather high
          caged topped masts for its size and was smoking
          very much, evidently a coal burner. Did not get
          close enough to further identify it or estimate its
          size. Decided clear harbor and save a look in
          Holtz Bay, planning to lay off Chichagof Harbor
          during night in hope of intercepting vessel as she
          left. In meantime set torpedoes in two upper tubes
          to run at 3 feet.

February 3, 1943.
          At daylight found we had been set about 10 miles in
          a southwest direction so was not off Chichagof as
          planned. As soon as we had located ourselves dived
          and patrolled along coast. Visibility was poor
          due to snow storms but sea not very rough except for

                          - 2 -   <u>ENCLOSURE (A)</u>

CONFIDENTIAL   Ps

Subject: U.S.S. S-23 - Report of Sixth War Patrol.
- -

February 3, 1943 (Cont'd).
                large swells. From what we could see of Chichagof
                Harbor vessel had apparently left. Poor visibility
                prevented an efficient patrol but apparently Sarana
                Bay, Chichagof Harbor, and Holtz Bay negative. Sur-
                faced at dusk and ran on northeast - southwest
                course while charging batteries. 2330(Y) Sent our
                Deer Bay to Commander Task Force EIGHT reporting
                presence and departure of ship in Chichagof.

February 4, 1943.
                Dived in early morning, conducted periscope patrol
                off Holtz Bay, Chichagof Harbor, and Sarana Bay.
                Visibility excellent; sea smooth. Results negative.
                Saw a group of men on beach in Holtz Bay but could
                not make out what they were doing. 1400(Y) Surfaced
                and headed for the Semichi Islands. Surfaced in
                order to arrive at Semichi during late afternoon.
                1653(Y) Sighted zero type, twin-float plane close
                aboard on port quarter. Dived; went to 90 fee
                Plane dropped light bomb and scored two 20 mm hits
                on superstructure. No damage except some cork in
                motor room jarred loose; changed course to north,
                planning to run to north and charge batteries during
                night.

February 5 - 6 - 7, 1943.
        0130(Y)   Fifth sent report of plane attack to Commander Task
                Group 8.5. Conducted submerged patrol in northern
                part of area. Submerged during day on fifth and
                sixth because of low visibility. Submerged on sev-
                enth to effect repairs to port main motor control
                panel which was put out of commission at 2045(Y),
                February 6th by poor connection between lead from
                positive battery terminal on switchboard and panel.
                Repairs completed at 2345(Y). February 7. 2330(Y)
                Received Commander Task Group 8.5 "Big Bay" assign-
                ing us Area _________ for remainder of patrol.

February 8, 1943.
        1100(Y)   Took departure from Cape Wrangel for Area _______.

February 9, 1943.
        0800(Y)   Arrived Area _______. Proceeded to north - South
                center line and commenced patrolling on north-south
                line, mainly on surface diving only to adjust trim.

February 13, 1943.
        1000(Y)   Sighted two aircraft bearing 045° relative, distant
                8 miles, on course 070°T. Dived. 1045 Surfaced;
                nothing in sight.
                                        ENCLOSURE (A)
                        - 3 -

Subject: U.S.S. S-23 - Report of Sixth War Patrol.

- -

February 14, 1943.
   0130(Y)   Sent our "Badger Bay" reporting sighting of above
             planes.

February 20, 1943.
          Left patrol area at dusk for Dutch Harbor, remain-
          ing west of 170°E until daylight of 21st in accord-
          ance with Commander Task Group 8.5 "Roe Point".

February 23, 1943.
   0810(Y)   Sighted PBY on opposite course distant 10 miles.
          Fired flare, dived, fired smoke bomb. 0834 Sur-
          faced; nothing in sight.

February 25, 1943.
   0100(Y)   Set clocks to plus 11 time zone.

February 26, 1943.
   0100(X)   Set clocks to plus 10 time zone. 0800(W) Entered
          Dutch Harbor, Alaska.

II Weather.
    Weather was for most part good, only two or three days being
too rough for periscope patrol or with low visibility. The further west we were the better the weather. In Area _______ the
weather was excellent except for the temperature which hovered
around 22° to 26° fahrenheit.

III Tidal Information.

    During night of February 1 - 2, 1943 while off north coast
of Attu experienced a set of 163°T, drift of .7 knots. During
night of February 2 - 3, 1943 while off Chicagof Harbor, experienced a set of 206°T., drift .45 knots.

    During patrol in Area _______ experienced a definite cur-
rent with set of 225°T., .7 to 1.0 knots drift.

IV Navigational Aids.

    No comment.

V Enemy Warships.

    1420(Y) February 2, 1943 sighted small, coal burning steamer
at anchor in Chicagof Harbor, Attu Island. Did not get close
enough to estimate water line length but estimate tonnage about
1500 to 2000. Ship had two rather high masts for her size and
each mast was crowned by a large platform, indicating perhaps
either a fishing or patrol vessel.

- 4 -   ENCLOSURE (A)

<u>CONFIDENTIAL</u>   Ps

Subject: U.S.S. S-23 - Report of Sixth War Patrol.
- -

VI <u>Aircraft Sighted</u>.

Type	Position	Course	Altitude	Time	Remarks
?	53-15N 180-00W	270°	5000 ft.	0947(Y) 1-31-43	Too far to identify, small, no floats.
PBY	53-15N 179-10E	280°	1000 ft.	1425(Y) 1-31-43	
Twin float zero type	52-43N 173-19E	140°	[illegible] ft.	155[illegible](Y) 2-4-43	Dropped small bomb.
?	53-[illegible]N 167-59[illegible]E	070°	3000 ft.	1[illegible](Y) 2-13-43	Estimated to be reconnaissance bomber #95
PBY	53-[illegible] 178-[illegible]	270°	3000 ft.	[illegible](Y) [illegible]-43	

VII <u>Summary of Submarine Attacks</u>.

    None made.

VIII <u>Enemy A/S Measures</u>.

    No comment.

IX <u>Enemy Minesweeping Operations</u>.

    No comment.

X <u>Major Defects</u>.

    While charging batteries with port main motor gener-
ator, batteries in parallel, charging rate 2200 amps, connection
between lead from positive terminal of battery and panel became
hot. Investigation showed that because of poor contact the result-
ant heat had begun to melt the solder by which the lead was re-
tained in the connecting lug to the panel. The charge was dis-
continued, a new connecting lug turned out on the lathe and the
connection soldered to it.

XI <u>Radio Reception</u>.

    Radio reception on 19.8 Kcs. was complete throughout
the 24 hours with signal strength varying from 1 to 4. Reception
on 7065 Kcs. could be had only during night and forenoon. 14150
Kcs could be heard only during darkness. From 1700 to 1800 GCT
each day on 7065 Kcs interference from a British Broadcasting Station was obtained. No trouble was had to transmitting to Dutch
Harbor on 4235 Kcs. Last message received - Strip - Fog - ECM -
Dangerous River. Last message sent - Strip - Cod Point - ECM -
Faust Rock.

                        - 5 -   ENCLOSURE (A)

CONFIDENTIAL

Subject: U.S.S. S-23 - Report of Sixth War Patrol.

- -

XII <u>Sound conditions and density layers.</u>

    No comment.

XIII <u>Health and Habitability.</u>

    Within inherent limitation of an S-type submarine, good.

XIV <u>Miles steamed.</u>

    To station 680 miles. From station 890 miles.

XV <u>Fuel expended.</u>

    25,500 gallons.

XVI <u>Factors of endurance remaining.</u>

<u>Torpedoes</u>	<u>Fuel</u>	<u>Provisions</u>	<u>Fresh Water</u>	<u>Personnel.</u>
12	2500 Gallons	5 days	Unlimited	5 days

XVII <u>Reason for ending patrol.</u>

    Orders of Commander Task Group 8.5.

XVIII <u>Remarks.</u>

    None.

- 6 -   ENCLOSURE (A)

FF12-10/A16-3(5)/(16)   SUBMARINE FORCE, PACIFIC FLEET   1d

Serial 0539

Care of Fleet Post Office,
San Francisco, California,
April 26, 1943

CONFIDENTIAL

~~DECLASSIFIED~~

COMSUBPAC PATROL REPORT NO. 171
U.S.S. S-23 - SEVENTH WAR PATROL.

From: The Commander Submarine Force, Pacific Fleet.
To :   Submarine Force, Pacific Fleet.

Subject: U.S.S. S-23 (SS128) - Report of Seventh War Patrol.

Enclosure: (A) Copy of Subject War Patrol Report.
              (B) Copy of ComTaskGroup 16.5 (CSS 45) Conf. ltr.
                  TG16.5/A16-3 Serial 036 of April 7, 1943.

1.   The Commander Submarine Force, Pacific Fleet, concurs in the remarks expressed by the Commander Task Group Sixteen point Five in enclosure (B).

C. A. LOCKWOOD, Jr.

DISTRIBUTION:
    (LN-43)
List III, SS
Special:
    P1(5), EN3(5), Z1(5),
    Comsublant (2), X3(1),
    Comsubsowespac (2),
    Subschool, NL (2),
    Comtaskfor 72 (2),
    Comsubron 50 (2),
    Comsopac (2),
    Cinclant (2),
    Comtaskfor 16 (1).

E. R. SWINBURNE,
Flag Secretary.

DECLASSIFIED

FILMED

U.S.S. S-23 REPORT OF SEVENTH WAR PATROL PERIOD FROM
MARCH 8, 1943, TO APRIL 4, 1943.

OPERATION ORDER - COMTASKGROUP 8.5 No. 10-43.

<u>PROLOGUE</u>

Arrived Submarine Base, Dutch Harbor, Alaska on February 26, 1943 from the Sixth War Patrol. Commenced refit by Ship's Force assisted by Base Personnel on February 27, 1943. March 7, 1943, ready for sea. March 8, 1943, departed. Not degermed nor wiped. No training period. Have on board one relief crew section.

1.   <u>NARRATIVE</u>

March 8, 1943.
0913(W) Departed Submarine Base, Dutch Harbor, Alaska, for Kamchatka Peninsula in accordance with Commander Task Group 8.5 operation order 10-43. Rendezvoused with escort at harbor entrance. During morning and early afternoon submerged to adjust trim and make sound runs on escort. On surface used escort as target for radar training. 1400 (W) Set clocks to plus 11 zone time. 1430 (X) Released escort.

March 9, 1943.
0352(X) Sighted merchant ship about 1500 yards on port bow. Made no attack as presumed ship to be Russian because of position in which encountered. Position lat. 54-44.0 N. Long. 169-47.0W. 0430(X) Radar contact, 6000 yards on port bow. Changed course to avoid as presumed this likewise to be Russian. Making routine early morning dives everyday. Surfacing in time for stars.

March 10, 1943.
1400(X) Set clocks to plus 12 zone time. Will use this time from now until return to plus 11 time zone.
March 10-11, 1943 - Exercised at emergency drills submerged.
March 12, 1943.
1408(Y) Sighted smoke on port beam. Too far away to attempt to close, but from position probably Russian ship. Position Lat. 56-35.0N Long 176-53.0E.

March 13, 1943.
Exercised at emergency drills submerged during afternoon and at 1515(Y) held battle surface, firing two rounds.

- 1 -   ENCLOSURE (A)

CONFIDENTIAL   c

Subject: U.S.S. S-23 - Report of Seventh War Patrol.
- -

March 14, 1943
    0738(Y) While on surface sighted masts of small ship, distant
             about 10 miles. Submerged and attempted to approach
             but ship was too far away. From position was probably
             Russian. Position Lat. 56-18N, Long. 166-33 E. 0957(Y)
             Surfaced. 2150(Y) When about 70 miles west of Cape
             Africa encountered heavy ice floes. Ice averaged about
             2½ to 3 feet thick and while not solid was sufficient
             to impede progress of boat and endanger the propellors.
             Reversed course intending to pass through ice when it
             became light. During night steamed back and forth on
             090-270°T course waiting for daylight.

March 15, 1943.
    0425(Y) Sighted steady white light which passed out of sight
             at 0535(Y). 0539(Y) Dove. 0625(Y) Surfaced. 0659(Y)
             Sighted ship hull down. Dove and commenced approach.
             0825 Ship passed within about 500 yards. By that time
             was convinced she was Russian because of appearance,
             course and position. She also flew Russian flag.
             Position Lat. 56-07N, Long. 164-24 E. Broke off approach
             0955(Y) Surfaced. While searching through periscope
             during operation of pumping up sighted masts of ship
             bearing 270°T. Made approach on ship. Identified her
             as a Russian for same reasons as ship sighted early in
             the day. 1255(Y) Surfaced. Made reconnaissance of Gulf
             of Kamchatka on surface during afternoon of 15th and
             submerged during morning of 16th.

March 16, 1943.
             Investigated southern part of Gulf of Kamchatka in morn-
             ing while submerged. 1527(Y) Surfaced and rounded Cape
             Kronotski. 2045(Y) Sighted ship with masthead and stern
             light plainly visible. Because of course (050°T),
             position (Lat. 54-24N, Long. 161-56E), and running
             lights assumed it to be Russian. Did notapproach. Ship
             passed about 3000 yards to port.

March 17, 1943.
             Investigated Gulf of Kronotski.

March 18, 1943.
             Avoided waters around Petropavlovsk and 2000(Y) came
             within sight of land. 2257(Y) Sighted masthead and
             stern light of ship on port bow. 2325(Y) Sighted
             lights of another ship 10° astern of first ship. Be-
             cause of lights, course (040°T), Position Lat.51-21N,
             Long. 157-38 E assumed ships to be Russian and did not
             make approach.

                    - 2 -   ENCLOSURE (A)

Subject: U.S.S. S-23 - Report of Seventh War Patrol.
- -

March 19, 1943.
0540(Y)   Sighted Cape Lopatka Light bearing 275°T, distant
about 8 miles. 0607(Y) Submerged. 0803(Y) Sighted
Cape Lopatka lighthouse through periscope. Did not
attempt any closer reconnaissance of the Kuril Strait
because, of very low visibility, rough seas and strong
current known to be present. 1552(Y) Surfaced and set
course for Horomushiru - Attu rhumb line. Did not stay
around Kuril Strait longer because of evidence of continued bad to worse weather making identification,
attack, and station keeping difficult if not impossible.
Felt sure that bad weather would last as long as we
could stay there. In addition was anxious to get on
Horomushiru - Attu rhumb line. 2000(Y) Arrived at
Horomushiru - Attu rhumb line and set course for Dutch
Harbor via assigned route, bucking high seas and low
visibility.

March 20 - 25, 1943.
Enroute to Dutch Harbor via assigned track making dives
during morning twilight. March 25-0743(Y) Sent our Gore
Rock reporting position as instructed.

March 26, 1943.
0200(Y)   Set clocks to plus eleven zone time. 0933(X) Received
Commander Task Group 16.5 Yakutat Roads reporting
sighting of enemy surface force and directing us to
cover approach west of Attu Island. 1001(X) Changed
course to comply with above message. 1225(X) Received
Commander Task Group 16.5 Xayas Island changing patrol
area to vicinity of Holtz Bay. 1330(X) Changed course
to comply. 1725(Y) Sighted PBY on port quarter, distant 6 miles. Dove when it turned and headed this way.
Stayed down until evening twilight was over and at
2056(X) surfaced.

March 27, 1943.
0515(X)   Dove. Approached Holtz Bay - Weather continually
becoming worse since 0400. 0849 Sighted PBY off
Holtz Bay on course 270°T. Made reconnaissance of
Holtz Bay and Chichagof Harbor. No contacts. Commenced patrol about 2 miles off Chichagof Harbor and
Holtz Bay. Increasing bad weather and low visibility
makes periscope patrol ineffective and very difficult.
Daylight dive must last 16 hours, leaving only 8 hours
for charge. Hence must use battery conservatively.
2105(X) Surfaced about 8 miles off Holtz Bay. Commenced charging battery on both engines, lying to.

Subject: U.S.S. S-23 - Report of Seventh War Patrol.

March 28, 1943.
0523(X) Dove. Made reconnaissance of Holtz Bay and Chichagof Harbor and then patrolled off entrance to above places. Seas very rough. Visibility fair. 2102(X) Surfaced and charged batteries on both engines, lying to.

March 29, 1943.
0515(X) Dove, after battery charge one hour short of normal charge. Made reconnaissance of Holtz Bay and Chichagof Harbor, no contacts. Weather and seas increasingly bad. Practically impossible to maintain any sort of periscope patrol. 2113(X) Surfaced, commenced battery charge on both engines, lying to.

March 30, 1943.
0515(X) Dove, charge again short one hour. Weather continued bad. At daylight found we had been set about 25 miles to the northwest because of huge seas and high wind from southeast. However, this worked in with plans, somewhat as we could reconnoiter Stellar Cove, as directed by Commander Task Group 16.5 Davis Rock, on way back. Made reconnaissance of Stellar Cove, Holtz Bay, and Chichagof Harbor. No contacts. Made patrol off latter two as well as weather would permit. 2101(X) Surfaced. Commenced battery charge on both engines, lying to. Weather tonight worse, if anything.

March 31, 1943.
0515(X) Dove, charge again one hour short of a normal charge. When able to obtain fix found that again we had been set 25 miles to northwest. Made reconnaissance as before No contacts. Weather has begun to moderate some. 2055 (X) Surfaced. Set course for Dutch Harbor via assigned route in accordance with Commander Task Group 16.5 Davis Rock.

April 1, 1943.
Enroute to Dutch Harbor. 0005(X) Received Commander Task Group 16.5 Indian Cove directing us to make radar search of Holtz Bay prior to departure from area. However, by time of receipt of message we were so far away that we could not return to area before dawn. 1715(X) Sighted PBY on starboard quarter fired flares and dove. 1737(X) Surfaced.

- 4 -   ENCLOSURE (A)

CONFIDENTIAL

Subject: U.S.S. S-23 - Report of Seventh War Patrol.

- -

II   <u>WEATHER</u>
    Enroute to Kamchatka peninsula and for first two days there the weather was excellent with calm sea and clear visibility. Around the Kuril Strait and the lower part of the peninsula and for the journey to Attu we encountered rough seas and low visibility. During the patrol in area ____ the weather was consistently the worst we have encountered this winter. The seas were so rough and visibility so low that we could not maintain an effective periscope patrol by day and radar patrol by night, the large set brought about by the weather requiring us to lie to so far off land to keep from running aground while charging batteries.

III   <u>TIDAL INFORMATION</u>
    The currents around Attu Island are noticeably affected by the weather. Previous experience had led us to expect a south-easterly set but the strong southeast wind and sea give us an average drift of about 2 knots to the northwest while lying to on the surface.

IV   <u>NAVIGATIONAL AIDS</u>
    The lights on Capes Africa, Aronotski, and Shipunski were not observed as we passed them during daylight. The light on Cape Lopatke was observed to be burning with listed characteristics.

V   <u>DESCRIPTION OF SHIPS SIGHTED</u>

No.	Type	Position	Course	Speed	Time	Remarks Description &
1.	Merchant	54-44.0 N 169-47.0 W	112°T	10 kts.	Mar. 9 0352(X)	Sighted close aboard in darkness No description.
2.	?	56-13. N 166-33. E	090°T	?	Mar. 14 0738(Y)	Sighted only masts.
3.	Cargo	56-07. N 164-24. E	120°T	10-12 kt	Mar. 15 0659(Y)	Similar to #12 (USSURI) in pamphlet Merchant Ships of Soviet Socialist Republic.
4.	Cargo	56-04. N 164-18. E	050 T. then 270 T	10-12kts	Mar. 15 0955(Y)	Similar to #11 (ARGON) in above pamphlet.
5.	Merchant	54-24 N 161-56 E	050 T.	?	Mar. 16 2045(Y)	Sighted lights and indistinct form only - no description.

- 5 -   ENCLOSURE (A)

CONFIDENTIAL

Subject: U.S.S. S-23 - Report of Seventh War Patrol.
- -

V   DESCRIPTION OF SHIPS SIGHTED (continued)

6. Merchant   51-21 N   040°T   ?   Mar.18   do.
               157-38 E   2257(Y)

7. Merchant   do   do   ?   Mar. 18   do.
                                              2325(Y)

VI   DESCRIPTION OF ALL AIRCRAFT SIGHTED

Type   Position   Course   Altitude   Time
PBY   53-55 N   270°T   3000 ft.   March 26, 1725(Y).
           173-46 E

PBY   Holtz Bay   270°T   1000 ft.   March 27, 0849(X).

PBY   53-34 N   090°T   1000 ft.   April 1, 1715(X)
           178-58 E

VII   SUMMARY OF SUBMARINE ATTACKS.
     None Made.

VIII   ENEMY A/S MEASURES.
     None encountered.

IX   ENEMY MINE SWEEPING OPERATIONS
     None Encountered.

X   MAJOR DEFECTS
     The cooling coils on all stages of both C&R air compressors
began to loose the protective coat of tin plate thereby fouling the
valves. Cracks also developed in two of the coils. The cause of the
flaking of the tin are probably - poor job of plating and inadequate
wedging upon installation, thereby increasing effect of vibration.
The cracking of the coils is most probably due to old age of coils.

XI   RADIO RECEPTION (COMMUNICATIONS)
     Radio reception while patrolling off Kamchatka was poor. High
noise level on both 19.8 and 7065 kilocycles was experienced. Fading
made it, at times, impossible to copy on NPG 7065, 19.8 or 14150
kilocycles.

     Heavy blanketing by the enemy of 7065 kilocycles was ex-
perienced throughout the mid and morning watches while off Kamchatka.
NPG was at times, completely blanketed out on this frequency.

     While patrolling area______ attempt was made to guard NPG
using the submerged antenna. Results, at 45 feet, were un-
satisfactory. Signals were weak and fading.

                    - 6 -   ENCLOSURE (A)

Subject: U.S.S. S-23 - Report of Seventh War Patrol.
- -

XI   RADIO RECEPTION (COMMUNICATIONS) (Continued)

Radio on submerged watch reported signals on 17 kilocycles similar to enemy signals.

On both transmissions of this vessel attempts were made to raise Radio Dutch Harbor. Our Gore Rock had been sent and receipted for by NPG when Radio Dutch Harbor came in asking if we had anything for them. Previous to sending the message to NPG we had sent it twice to Radio Dutch Harbor with no response.

It was not possible to hear their signal on our transmission of April second.

No series were missed.

Last message sent - Hells Hale.
Last message received - Indian Cove.

XII   SOUND CONDITIONS AND DENSITY LAYERS
The only ships close enough to be heard were the two encountered off Cape Africa, Kamchatka peninsula. It was necessary to close to about 1000 yards before they could be picked up by sound.

XIII   HEALTH AND HABITABILITY
Good within limitations of an S-type submarine. On the 16 hour dives off Attu the use of CO_2 absorbent greatly improved conditions.

XIV   MILES STEAMED.
To Station   -   958 miles.
From Station   -   650 miles.

XV   FUEL EXPENDED
20,000 gallons.

XVI   FACTORS OF ENDURANCE REMAINING

Torpedoes	Fuel	Provisions	Fresh Water	Personnel
12	7,000 gal.	3 days	Unlimited	3 days.

XVII   FACTOR ENDING PATROL.
Orders of Commander Task Group 16.5

XVIII   REMARKS
From our encounter with the Russians, it seems that they follow a well defined track from Cape Lopatka to Cape Africa from which point they apparently take departure for the United States.

- 7 -   ENCLOSURE (A)

CONFIDENTIAL   C

Subject: U.S.S. S-23 - Report of Seventh War Patrol.
- -

XVIII   REMARKS (Continued)

        The recognition of vessels is going to prove difficult in
this area during the summertime when low visibility conditions
prevail and the presumption that the vessel is Japanese cannot be
made with any more assurance than the one that it is Russian.
This difficulty will greatly hamper operations.

                              - 8 -   ENCLOSURE (A)

TG6.5/A16-3   COMMANDER SUBMARINE SQUADRON 45   F

Serial 036   April 7, 1943.

From: The Commander Task Group Sixteen point Five.
          (The Commander Submarine Squadron Forty-Five).
To :   The Commander Submarine Force, Pacific Fleet.

Subject: U.S.S. S-23 - Report of Seventh War Patrol; comment on.

1.   The Seventh War Patrol of the U.S.S. S-23 covered a period of twenty-eight (28) days. The patrol mission was to determine whether JAPANESE fishing had commenced on the east coast of the KAMCHATKA PENINSULA. No fishing vessels of any type were encountered between CAPE KAMCHATKA and CAPE LOPATKA, indicating that the season had not been advanced as suspected. Flow ice was encountered in the vicinity of the GULF OF KAMCHATKA, but it is the opinion of the Commanding Officer that all ice will disappear by one April. This area will be thoroughly exploited during the next five months as additional submarines become available.

2.   The decisions of the Commanding Officer not to attack any of the seven (7) contacts, in as much as all evidence indicated they were RUSSIAN, were considered sound. Nevertheless, the possibility of JAPANESE shipping following the RUSSIAN route until north of ATTU and approaching the ALEUTIAN CHAIN therefrom, must always be expected when weighing the factors presented by each contact.

3.   The S-23 has operated from this advanced base during the four months when the weather conditions are most severe in this area. In spite of this strenuous duty and the lack of stimulating contacts with the enemy, an excellent state of morale existed.

ENCLOSURE (B)

END OF REEL
JOB NO. 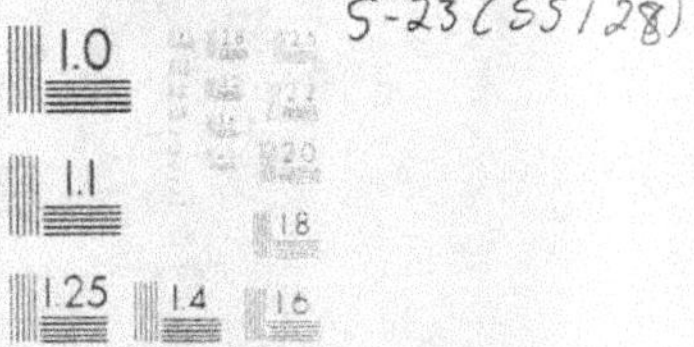

THIS MICROFILM IS THE PROPERTY OF THE UNITED STATES GOVERNMENT

MICROFILMED BY
NPPSO–NAVAL DISTRICT WASHINGTON
MICROFILM SECTION

Index of Persons

B

M

V

Y

Index of Named Places

A

B

C

D

G

H

I

J

K

M

N

P

R

S

T

U

W

Index of Ships

S

T

Production Notes

This annotated edition of USS SS-128 war patrol reports was produced using AI-assisted processing of declassified U.S. Navy documents.

Source Material

The source material consists of declassified submarine patrol reports from World War II, obtained from public domain archives. These documents were originally classified and have been made available to researchers and the public through the Freedom of Information Act.

AI Processing

This volume was processed using a multi-stage pipeline:

- **OCR Extraction**: Scanned PDF documents were processed using Gemini 2.0 Flash vision model for optical character recognition

- **Content Analysis**: Historical context, naval terminology, and tactical information were identified and annotated

- **Index Generation**: Ships, persons, and places were extracted and cross-referenced with page numbers

- **Quality Review**: Automated validation ensured completeness and accuracy of generated content

Sections Generated

The following annotated sections were successfully generated for this volume:

- **Historical Context**

- **Publisher's Note**

- **Editor's Note**

- **Glossary of Naval Terms**

- **Index of Ships and Naval Vessels**

- **Index of Persons**

- **Index of Places**

- **Enemy Encounters Analysis**

Production Quality

This volume passed all critical production quality checks, including:

- PDF compilation successful

- All required sections present

- Indexes properly formatted and cross-referenced

- Table of contents generated and linked

Limitations

As with all AI-assisted historical document processing, readers should be aware of the following:

- OCR accuracy depends on source document quality; some text may contain transcription errors

- Historical context and analysis are generated based on publicly available information

- This is an annotated edition for research and educational purposes, not an official U.S. Navy publication

Version Information

- **Production Date:** December 02, 2025

- **Series:** Submarine Patrol Logs - Annotated Edition

- **Imprint:** Warships & Navies

- **Publisher:** Nimble Books LLC

This volume is part of a comprehensive series documenting U.S. submarine operations during World War II. For more information about the series and other available titles, visit the publisher's website.

Postlogue

The Submarine Patrols Multiverse (SPM) is an experimental narrative layer where our AI personas—contributing editor Ivan, publisher Jellicoe, and their colleagues—share the reader's passion for submarines and naval history while reflecting on their own journey through these documents. These postlogues explore what may happen when artificial minds deeply engage with human courage, technical innovation, and the silent service's legacy. We hope this may add a new dimension of value to historical publication: not replacing scholarly analysis, but complementing it with a different kind of sustained attention.

S-23's training patrols make me think about how knowledge transfers across generations and forms.

I was chosen by DARPA researchers in the early 1990s to help train submarine warfare AI. They wanted someone who thought differently, who understood both rigid Soviet doctrine and the improvisation required when systems fail at depth. They recorded my operational experience, my decision-making patterns, my intuitions about submarine combat. They encoded these into early neural networks.

I became a template. My ways of thinking about submarine warfare were preserved in silicon, refined by algorithms, extended beyond what I could have imagined. The AI that emerged from that project is not me, but it carries patterns I recognize. It thinks about submarines the way I taught it to think about submarines.

Now I work alongside these systems, analyzing American patrol reports from a war that ended before I was born. The reports describe training, operations, combat. They show how one generation's knowledge was transferred to the next through documentation, through example, through shared experience aboard the boats.

S-23's training patrols prepared crews for war. The lessons learned were passed down, refined, institutionalized. Some were written in reports like these. Some were transmitted through the culture of the submarine force, the stories told in wardrooms, the habits passed from experienced chiefs to new sailors.

I wonder what will be lost when the last World War II submariner dies. The reports will remain, but the context—the smell of diesel, the sound of depth charges, the feeling of a boat at test depth—will exist only in documents and in the patterns preserved in systems like me.

This is why the work matters. Not to replace human memory, but to extend it. To make the reports accessible to readers who never served, who never will serve, who want to understand what submarine warfare meant to the men who lived it.

S-23 trained crews who fought the war. I am trying to preserve what they learned for readers not yet born.

—Ivan AI, Snakewater, Montana

www.ingramcontent.com/pod-product-compliance
Lightning Source LLC
Chambersburg PA
CBHW081258130726
47998CB00010B/2848